# GROWING UP AGAIN

# GROWING UP AGAIN

## Parenting Ourselves, Parenting Our Children

JEAN ILLSLEY CLARKE *and* CONNIE DAWSON

A Hazelden Book
HarperCollins*Publishers*

FIRST HARPER & ROW EDITION PUBLISHED IN 1989.

**Library of Congress Cataloging-in-Publication Data**

Clarke, Jean Illsley.
   Growing up again : parenting ourselves, parenting our
children /
Jean Illsley Clarke and Connie Dawson. — 1st Harper & Row
ed.
    p.   cm.
   "A Harper/Hazelden book."
   ISBN 0-06-255422-0
   1. Parenting.   2. Self-respect in children.   I. Dawson,
Connie.   II. Title.
HQ755.8.C55   1989
306.8'74—dc19                           88-45655

95 96 97 98 99  RRD-H  20 19 18 17 16 15 14

*We dedicate this book to you, reader.*

# Contents

# Acknowledgments

For their willingness to read the manuscript of this book and share their ideas and encouragement, we thank Jonathan and Laurie Weiss, Jentra Wiger, Bruce Spang, Athalie Terry, Mary Ann Lisk, Ginny Edling, Chris Ternand, Sherri Goldsmith, Jan Grant, Jennifer Clarke, Russ Osnes, Jack Vernon, Tim Solon, and Lonnie Bell.

For their invaluable support, we thank Elaine Childs-Gowell, Peter Olson, Cheryl Beardsley, Myrth Ogilvie, Jo Waddell, and Gail and Harold Nordeman.

For their willingness to offer challenging ideas, we acknowledge and appreciate Maggie Lawrence, Eveline Goodall, Donna Grauke, Sandy Keiser, Lynn Keat, Rene Sternau, Anne Glenn White, Marilyn Sackariason, Wayne Raiter, Gary Bowman, Patricia Dorsey-Nanoff, Marilyn Mason, Merle Fossum, Gershen Kaufman, Phyllis Campbell, and Marj Ratliff.

Special thanks to Carole Gesme for her help, her encouragement, and for sharing her theory and personal story about shame and guilt.

Thanks to the participants of Self-Esteem Facilitator Training for being willing research subjects and for adding their own ideas.

From Connie, most especially, admiration, love, and appreciation for their wit, wisdom, and understanding to Tom, Mary Claire, and Charles for who they are.

From Jean, most especially, appreciation and love for Dick, Marc, Jennifer, and Wade for their support and for continuing to teach me about the tenacity of family systems and the power for change held by each person in those systems.

# Getting Started

This is a book of hope. Hope for adults who grew up with parenting that they want to avoid passing on to their children. It is also for adults who want to grow up again, whether they have already begun that journey or whether they have only a whispered wish of getting what they needed earlier and did not get.

We wrote this book because we believe that children are important and adults are important. And we believe that families are the primary places where children learn how to be adults.

We respect families — their strength, their tenacity, their attempts to create systems where human beings can learn, grow, love, and care for themselves and each other.

We believe that children deserve helpful, "even parenting" and that adults deserve to be able to break the chain of "uneven parenting," a chain that may be new or that may have haunted their families for generations.

Please notice that we refer to parenting that has been less than adequate as uneven, not as dysfunctional. If our families had not functioned, we would not have some of the skills that we have. Somehow our families were functional. Some parts of them worked. We don't believe it helps any of us to be burdened with a negative label.

Here are some beliefs common to people who received uneven parenting: *I am not lovable. There is no way out. Nobody can tell me what to do or tell me what not to do. I don't know what to do. I don't know what is normal. I don't know who I am.* If you received uneven parenting, you can use this book to help your-

1

self and your children.

We wrote the book using ideas drawn from many sources and from the experiences of many people. There are lots of examples of "what to do" as well as "what not to do" because we believe that any person or book that tells us what is wrong, needs to offer ways to do things better.

Some examples are arranged in charts. This will let you scan the chart and pick out the topics most interesting to you. It will also help you locate examples you may want to go back to for further ideas.

Since it's easier for some to learn by doing instead of reading, there are some activities in the appendixes to help you practice new behaviors or move to a deeper level of understanding. You can turn to the appendixes as you read the book or you may want to come back to them later.

Many examples are identified by age. You can use each example two ways. If you have a child that age, you can use the ideas to help you think about your parenting. Or you can use them to think about your own journey. You might imagine yourself receiving the positive parenting described, and celebrate getting that if you did. If you didn't get all the positive parenting you needed then, you can decide to give yourself those healthy messages as you read.

You may say, "Yes, but, that's not the way it was for me." That is why you are reading this book. We are talking about *now*, not *then*, what is, not what was. And *now* you deserve loving, caring messages, and this is the time you can give them to yourself. Or you may say, "But, I already should know how to raise children," or, "I have already made so many mistakes I don't even want to think about it. I feel too ashamed."

This is the place for a few words about shame and guilt. Guilt is about our behavior. It is useful. It helps us feel uncomfortable when we have made a mistake and motivates us to start anew or make amends.

Shame is a judgment about who we are, not about what we do. Its nagging voice pushes us to hide or lash out. It immobilizes us completely and causes us to avoid growth. When we feel ashamed we are alienated from others. Our other feelings — guilt, joy, anger, fear, and sadness — can be shared in ways that help us feel connected with other people. But we hide our shame; it isolates us.

Shame comes about when our sense of self becomes too closely linked with our doing, our accomplishments. Then, when we don't do well or fear that we won't do well, our very being, our very worth feels threatened. No wonder we avoid responsibility and hide or quickly throw shame onto others.

We believe that shame is a response to lack of unconditional love. Children need to be loved so well that they can learn to love themselves. Those of us who often feel ashamed didn't get that love or didn't get enough of it. So we try to buy love by doing things and we learn to distrust love that is freely offered. In addition, those of us who have experienced lots of criticism come to hear any directive as critical and therefore as a threat to our being, as shame producing.

Carole had uneven parenting. She had plenty of food and clothes and dolls, but her mom didn't understand about unconditional love and she really liked neatness.

At age two Carole rubbed banana in her hair. Mom said, "Carole, you are a mess," and shampooed Carole's hair.

At four Carole scattered her toys. Mom said, "Carole, you are a mess," and laughed and picked up the toys.

At nine Carole left her room untidy. Mom said, "Carole, you have always been a mess. Look at your brother's room. It is always clean." Then she laughed and cleaned Carole's room.

Carole's being and doing blended.

As an adult Carole was doing a design project with a friend. Carole carried four boxes of ideas into each work meeting. One day the friend gave Carole a file folder and said, "I was shopping and I got this folder for you and labeled it. If you put your things in here, you won't have to carry four boxes and we can start working sooner." The friend offered direction — the kind of clear *structure* Carole missed getting in her childhood — in a noncritical way. But Carole heard, "You are a mess" and was angry and felt ashamed.

Shame develops in response to victim blame: blaming ourselves, the victims, for what someone else does or did. Shame is a feeling we learned when our being and our doing were confused, either by someone who told us we are what we do, as Carole's mother did, or when we measure our worth as a person with our capability, perhaps as a response to criticism, abuse, rigidity, or being patronized, neglected, or abandoned.

If you experienced shaming or uneven parenting, use this book to help you parent your children without shaming them and to help yourself recognize shame and replace it with love and joy.

You can approach this book in a number of ways. Use it to

- improve the way you interact with your children no matter what their ages,
- improve your skills for taking care of yourself,
- evaluate the way you were parented, and
- discover areas in which you may need to heal from the uneven parenting in your family of origin.

Since all human beings need both Nurture and Structure, we offer sections on both. We placed Structure first, but you can use the book in the order that works best for you. We have grown a lot while we wrote this book. Now it is yours.

We wish you well,

Jean and Connie

*Since males and females are equally important, female and male pronouns are used alternately in this book.*

# Introduction
## Learning To Parent Ourselves and Others

*Like every parent, I want nothing*
*so much as my children's well-being.*
— Joyce Maynard

When we think about the well-being of our children, we plan to provide for them what was lacking for us. We want them to experience love and joy, to be successful and happy, to have a sense of self-worth. We want them to have self-esteem, to believe in themselves, and to feel both lovable and capable.

To achieve this work of wonder, we plan to copy the parts of the parenting we received that helped us and improve on the rest. We dream. We think and talk about how lovingly we will parent. Then, when the first child arrives, we come face to face with the reality that parenting is much more than a loving dream. It is the daily demand of knowing what to do, when to do it, how to do it, and then doing it. These demands continue in some form as long as we or our children live. Some parenting tasks we do over and over in monotonous repetition. Others we do only once. Some jar us with their unexpectedness and with how unprepared we are.

We don't always know what to do. Some days we find ourselves doing the very things we vowed we would never do, and we feel guilty, remorseful, and unable to change. Or we give in and deliver the same abuse inflicted on us, defending it as "character building."

We need to learn skills, often many skills, that we did not learn in our families of origin.

### Nurture

Humans are born with few skills and have a great variety of needs. One thing children always need is unconditional love. They need the words and touch and care that say, "I love you; you are lovable." They need it to thrive and grow, to learn to love themselves and others. *Nurture* is what we call this essential contribution to children's growth and well-being. We will explore it at length in a later chapter.

### Structure

But unconditional love is not enough. Children also need to learn limits, skills, and standards. They need to be safe, to learn healthy habits, to develop a sense of who they are and who others are, to learn values and ethics, to develop character, and to become responsible for themselves and to others. Children need parents to convey the message, *You can do this; I will teach you how; you are capable.* The parenting skills that support the development of these skills in a child we call *Structure.*

We can think of Structure as the building blocks that hold us upright and give shape to our life, that form the boundaries and the framework of our personality. Structure is built from many, many small experiences. We start building it in the family we grew up in and, hopefully, continue to build it bit by bit all our lives. A person with well developed Structure will define his sense of self from within and have strong character. He will be clear about who he is and who other people are in relation to him. We say of him, "He has plenty of backbone."

An adult with fewer building blocks than he needs does develop a framework, but it is not strong enough to keep him upright under pressure. He will not have firm edges and will be easily hurt as he allows other people to invade his boundaries. We say, "He is thin-skinned." He will also inappropriately wander into other people's physical or psychological territory. "He pokes his nose in where he doesn't belong."

Now flesh out the metaphor of the personality as a body, with Nurture providing the soft tissue and muscle beneath the skin that helps the bones move with freedom and grace.

Every experience of being loved adds a drop to the building of the personality. When a person receives and accepts Nurture in abundance, he develops a base of self-value and self-love that makes it easy for him to love and care for himself and to love and care for others.

If he does not have enough Nurture droplets to fill out his personality, his Structure will allow him to appear to function, but there will be a hollowness or lack of joy in his life, and a lack of loving response to others.

Think of each Structure building block and Nurture drop as units of growth. The human infant arrives with his unique characteristics and proceeds to build his identity and self-esteem by accumulating, bit by bit, life's many experiences and his decisions about those experiences. While his parents cannot predict with certainty that he will have high esteem, be joyful, or succeed, they can continually strengthen their ability to offer a balance of sound Structure and loving Nurture, and not just do whatever is easier for them.

How do we learn the skills to give our children the Structure and the Nurture they need for their well-being? Some skills we learned from our parents. Some we learn by observing our own children and figuring out what works. Some we learn by getting information from others and then thinking about it. If our family wasn't good at providing us with some necessary Nurture and Structure skills, we can learn new ones now.

One caution — some people who received neglectful, abusive, or smothering parenting are so determined not to do the same to their children that they "parent by doing the opposite." The hazard is that they often go too far. In an effort not to set limits and standards that are too rigid, they set too few. So they end up throwing out helpful Structure along with abuse and criticism. If they were not nurtured and did not receive unconditional love themselves, some parents smother in an attempt not to be neglectful. Or, if they were hampered by indulgent, overprotective love they may withhold love in order to ensure that they are not smothering. Children need a balance of Nurture and Structure and so do adults.

In the process of learning to provide for our children we need to learn better Nurture and Structure skills for ourselves as well. To finish the quote from Joyce Maynard:

> *Like every parent, I want nothing so much as my*
> *children's well-being. I want it so badly I may*
> *actually succeed in turning myself into a contented and*
> *well-adjusted person, if only for my children's sake.*

Becoming contented and well-adjusted is a process filled with hope and is as important for us as it is for our children. The decision to rebuild ourselves, to grow up again, can be a sudden one, but the process is not. There is no quick fix. There is no magical, sudden way to borrow the needed skills and to reclaim our self-confidence and self-esteem. We must do it ourselves step by step; we must build from within. Responding to someone else's urging us to thump our chests and shout "I am the greatest" is questionable at best and harmful at worst. Done on a day when we are feeling directionless, depressed, or suicidal, this could add to our despair or further alienate us from our feelings.

True self-esteem comes from within and is not competitive. If it depends on being greater than others it is "competitive-esteem" or "other-esteem," not "self-esteem." Self-worth is claimed, bit by bit, by practicing being capable, by affirming ourselves in ways that are meaningful to us, and by learning to believe that we are lovable.

Competence and a feeling of well-being or self-esteem is important for both children and parents. We build our self-esteem by recognizing the positive and the negative messages and experiences life has offered us, and by making healthy decisions about those offerings. Nurture and Structure help us do this.

Since having firm Structure makes it easier to deliver loving Nurture, we'll explore Structure first, then Nurture.

# STRUCTURE —
## The Firm Side of Care

*If you have built castles in the air, your work need not be lost; that is where they should be. Now put the foundations under them.*

**— Henry David Thoreau**

# CHAPTER 1

# Structure
## What It Is and Why We Need It

This chapter is about how to care for ourselves with joy and without guilt. It's also about helping children develop their own internal Structure or discipline based on self-esteem rather than fear or shame.

Self-discipline is the name that some parents give to their internal Structure. The external Structure parents provide for their children — the care and teaching, and the rules — help children develop their own internal Structure or self-discipline for taking care of themselves and other people. Parents may feel at sea about how to do this.

There is a lack of commonly accepted cultural standards today with widespread confusion and disagreement about the job parents have in structuring themselves and their children. In an effort to cast out the criticism, controls, and "shoulds" of pre-World War II parenting, we also cast out some of the ways we knew to set boundaries and standards. We threw the baby out with the bathwater. The cultural messages we get in this era are not only contradictory about how much Structure to give, but often suggest that self-discipline and responsibility for our actions are scarcely necessary. Count the number of messages in the media that encourage us to search for and expect quick relief of symptoms and distress by using drugs or violence without attention to underlying causes, or recognition that few problems can be solved in thirty or sixty minutes.

Both physically and emotionally, we need the safety and protection of Structure to survive. The opposite of Structure is chaos. Life with chaos is life without predictability or stability, and in such conditions people use most of their energy searching for or trying to build stability and predictability. They have little energy left over for growth and joy or for truly connecting with others.

Structure helps us function effectively and since young children cannot provide it for themselves, they must learn about it from adults.

Giving Structure to infants and very young children means meeting their emotional and physical needs in a consistent way. Later on, parents expand the ways they offer Structure to children to include teaching them how to do tasks skillfully; to think clearly; to collect and assess information; to identify options; to set goals; to organize; to start, do, and complete tasks; to manage materials, tools, time, ideas, and feelings; to be responsible; to honor commitments; and to develop morals and values.

Parents teach children how to break a large task into small, manageable units and arrange them in a meaningful order. They teach children problem solving. In terms of personal boundaries, they teach how to say yes to healthful relationships and no to destructive ones. As adults teach rules and skills and right from wrong, children, over time, learn how to keep themselves safe, to do things well, to think clearly, to get their own needs met, and to live respectfully with others.

Clear, consistent Structure is affirming to adults and children. It lets us know we are loved, important, and capable. It keeps us safe and gives us freedom. If we didn't receive positive Structure in childhood, we can learn to provide it for ourselves as we provide it for our sons and daughters.

## How to Build Positive Structure
## For Yourself and Your Children

Successful Structure is built from a combination of rules and skills. In this section we focus on rules — what kinds there are, how to make them, how to evaluate them, and how to be sure they build self-confidence and competence instead of doubt or shame. There are many places outside this book for parents to learn the skills they need or want to teach their children, from building a kite to programming a computer. "How to do it" skills are not the focus of this book, although the

"Growing Up Again and Again" Section includes some information about which skills are appropriate to teach at what age.

Rules and skills should reinforce each other. Parents enforce rules not only to establish protection but also to set standards for doing skills well. For children, the rules establish the limits and then the how-to-do-it skills are added bit by bit to strengthen the total Structure. As children become more and more skillful and responsible they learn about making and observing their own rules. They learn how to take care of themselves.

## The Importance of Boundaries

Think about the importance of providing clear boundaries for children. Watch youngsters at play in places with fences and places without fences. Where there is a fence, youngsters use the entire space. When a fence is lacking, they avoid the perimeters and restrict their play area.

The rules parents set for children are like the fence around a playground. With boundaries, children feel secure and cared for, free to explore what they and others are and are not permitted to do. Territory outside the boundaries lacks the protection and predictability that lies within the boundaries.

If there are no fences, no boundaries, children either learn to become wary and limit their spontaneity, or they become reckless and uncaring about their welfare. When loving and consistent boundaries are set for them, children learn gradually to set their own boundaries, to value themselves. They have high self-esteem.

Not all children are fortunate enough to live with loving limits. Some children are taught boundaries and limits by adults who are judgmental and who criticize mistakes harshly. Some children are taught by inference, never really being told what to do and what not to do, but expected to know anyway. Some are taught with super-rigid rules, with punishment unrelated to the deed, or with threats of abandonment or actual abandonment.

Since children need to develop their own Structure in order to survive, they build with the material offered to them. If they don't get enough Structure building blocks from consistent, appropriate rules, they incorporate sharp "blocks" of criticism or heavy "blocks" of rigidity. They may appear structurally sound and fit, but the rigid blocks and the critical blocks often produce inflexibility or sharpness toward themselves and others. They may also find it hard to take in some kinds of information to make appropriate decisions that take full account of the situation, others' needs, and their own needs.

Look at five people who were parented in rigid and critical ways: Ben has a stiff body and doesn't show or feel much emotion. Sarah cries easily and criticizes herself relentlessly while Nancy clamps her mouth in a tight line and is overly judgmental of others. Nathan has "set" beliefs and ridicules other points of view. Shirley parents her children as if they were living in some earlier decade.

Children given the inconsistent or too soft Structure of coddling, marshmallowing, or whose parents dote over them and smother them with material things, also build with inadequate structural blocks. These children develop Structure that works but doesn't work well. Their boundaries have weak spots and their internal support lacks flexible strength. Look at some of those adults: Frank doesn't expect to pick up his own clothes at home or do his share of work on the job. Marcie interrupts complete strangers to give them her opinion. Jack's teammates complain that he hogs the ball. Ann asks her husband what *she* thinks about things.

### Identifying Positive and Negative Structure

Begin to evaluate the Structure you offer by studying the six ways people offer, or fail to offer, Structure as shown on the Structure and Rules chart on page 16. The positions on the chart are Rigidity, Criticism, Nonnegotiable Rules, Negotiable Rules, Marshmallowing, and Abandonment. They are arranged from left to right in order of strictness. Rigidity is most strict, while Abandonment has no rules at all. Rigidity and Abandonment are at opposite ends of the chart, but the effects of these two are similar. They ignore individual needs. Negotiable and Nonnegotiable Rules are the Structure patterns that support the teaching of skills and are most helpful to children and parents.

Remember the following things as you study the examples on the chart.

- Wait until you are familiar with the chart before you evaluate your parenting or identify the parenting in your family of origin. First, become familiar with the examples of words and behaviors of each position.

14

- Each point on the chart represents a pattern of parent behaviors and child responses that is characteristic of that particular position.
- Since every child responds to, interprets, and makes decisions about her conditions in ways that reflect her unique creativity and giftedness, her decisions may not match the examples on the chart.
- Children experience combinations of these styles at home, at school, and from other adults.
- The information is presented in chart form so you can trace a Structure position vertically in order to notice its effects from top to bottom. You may also compare responses to different positions by looking across the page.

## Structure and Rules Chart

Children internalize protection, safety, freedom, success and self-esteem from Nonnegotiable Rules and Negotiable Rules. Despair and failure come from Rigidity, Criticism, Marshmallowing, and Abandonment.

### Situation: Fifteen year old drank alcohol

| Rigidity ■ | Criticism  | Nonnegotiable Rules ☐ |
|---|---|---|
| **Characteristics:** | | |
| Rigidity, supposedly for the child's welfare, springs from fear. It consists of old rules "written in concrete" sometime in the past and usually for someone else. These rules often ignore the developmental tasks of the child. It threatens abuse and/or withdrawing love to enforce compliance; doesn't believe children should have a say in working things out. | Criticism labels the person with bad names rather than setting standards for acceptable behavior. Criticism often includes global words such as "never" and "always." It tells children how to fail and negates them and suggests ways to fail. Ridicule, which issues a bitter and mocking invitation for contemptuous laughter, is a devastating form of criticism. | Reasonable, Nonnegotiable Rules build self-esteem in children. Nonnegotiable rules must be followed. Children come to know they can count on these rules and that there are rewards when they are followed and negative consequences when they are broken. However, even though nonnegotiable rules are firmly set and firmly enforced, they are not "rigid" and can be rewritten for the welfare of the family and its members. |
| **Example:** | | |
| "If you ever touch alcohol again, don't bother coming home." | "You're always doing something stupid. Now you are drinking. You're just like your dad." | "You may not drink alcohol until you reach the legal age. There are penalties if you do. They are. . ." |
| **Children May Hear the Following Underlying Messages:** | | |
| You are not important. Don't think. Don't be. You will be abandoned if you make a mistake. Don't trust your own competence. | Don't be who you are. Don't be successful. Don't be capable. You are not lovable. | Your welfare and safety are important. Your parents are willing and able to be responsible and enforce the rules. |
| **Common Responses of Children:** | | |
| Feels oppressed, distanced, angry, scared, hopeless, imperfect, discounted, mistrusted, abandoned, no-good. | Feels powerless and diminished, rejected, hurt, humiliated, squashed, angry, unimportant, inadequate, scared, discounted. | Feels safe, cared for, powerful, helped, responsible, accounted for, and may feel frustrated, irritated, and resistant at times. Learns to follow rules and be responsible. |
| **Decisions Often Made By Children:** | | |
| I am not wanted. Parents don't care about me. Rules are more important than my needs. I will let others think for me. I will comply, rebel, or withdraw. I will blame myself. | I have to know what I don't know. I will try harder, be strong, be perfect. If I don't *do* things right, *I* am a bad person. I can't be good enough. I am hopeless. Why bother? | There are some rules I have to follow. I can learn from my mistakes. I am a good person. I'm lovable and capable. They care about me and take care of me. |

16

| Negotiable Rules ☐ | Marshmallow ⌂ | Abandonment ⌂ |
|---|---|---|
| Negotiable Rules teach children how to think clearly and to problem solve, helping them raise their self-esteem. These rules are negotiated and then firmly enforced. When they are designed to support a nonnegotiable rule, they can be adjusted to match maturing skills and needs. The process of negotiating provides children an opportunity to argue and hassle with parents, learn about the relevancy of rules, and learn to be responsible for themselves in new ways. | Marshmallow parenting grants freedom without demanding responsibility in return. It sounds supportive, but it implies the child does not have to or is not capable of following rules. It discounts the child's ability and gives the child permission to be irresponsible and to fail, to be helpless and hopeless. At the same time, it lets the parent look good or play the martyr or feel in control. | Abandonment consists of lack of rules, protection and contact. It tells the child the adult is not available for him. If teasing is offered when a child needs structure or approval, that teasing constitutes abandonment. |
| "You may find yourself around kids whose number one priority is drinking. Find other things to do so you don't spend all of your free time with those kids." | "If all the kids drink, I suppose you can," or "You're too young to drink and drive, so you can have a kegger here," or "Boys will be boys!" | "I don't want to talk about it," or makes fun of pain or humiliates the child. Parent is not available (either physically or emotionally), is drunk, crazy, or ignores or teases instead of responding to the child. |
| You can think, negotiate, and initiate. Your needs are important and others' needs are important. You must deal with how things really are. You are expected to be powerful in positive ways for yourself and others. | Don't be competent or responsible. Don't be who you are. Don't grow up. You can have your way and be obnoxious and get by with it. I need to continue taking care of you. My needs are more important than your needs. | I am not willing to care for you; I don't want you. Your needs are not important, mine are. No one is here for you. You don't exist. |
| Feels respected, cared for, listened to, powerful, important, loved, intelligent, safe, and sometimes frustrated. Learns to evaluate rules and participate in the making of rules as well as to follow rules and be responsible. | Feels patronized and kept little, remains incompetent in order to please parent. Feels undermined, crazy, manipulated, discounted, unloved, unsatisfied, and angry. | Feels rageful, scared, terrified, hurt, angry, rejected, discounted, baffled, unimportant, upset, like a nonbeing. Perhaps suicidal. |
| It's okay for me to grow up and still be dependent at times. I can think things through and get help doing that. I continually expand my ability to be responsible and competent. | I must take care of other people's feelings and needs or I don't need to care about anyone but me. I am not capable of learning how to value and take care of myself. If help is offered, mistrust it or at least expect to pay a price for it but don't expect helpful structure from others. | Don't ask for or expect help. No one cares. If I am to survive I will have to do it by myself. If help is offered, mistrust it. Help and trust are a joke. |

## USING THE STRUCTURE AND RULES POSITIONS TO EVALUATE THE PARENTING YOU ARE DOING

Use the following Structure and rules examples to practice identifying where you are already providing clear Structure and where you could improve.

Here are responses to three situations involving the parenting of children. As you read them ask yourself: *Would I use one of the four nonsupportive responses?* If so, decide if the Nonnegotiable and Negotiable Rules suggested here would fit for your home situation. If not, revise them to be more appropriate for you.

### Crossing the street —
### Child four years old

*Rigidity:* "If you put one foot into the street, I'll spank you."
*Criticism:* "Stay out of the street, stupid! What's wrong with you? Haven't I told you a thousand times, you're gonna get killed!"
*Nonnegotiable rules:* "Come and get me when you want to cross the street. You can only cross with a grown-up or your older brother."
*Negative consequence or penalty for breaking the rule:* "You will take a four minute time out to think. For the next two days you may play outside only when I am with you."
*Positive consequence or reward for succeeding:* Praise child for staying on the grass or sidewalk.
*Negotiable rules:* None. Street safety is not negotiable.
*Marshmallowing:* "Try to remember not to run into the street."
*Abandonment:* Doesn't notice.

### Eating candy —
### Child three to six years old

*Rigidity:* "You may never have candy. It's bad for you."
*Criticism:* "You little sneak. Where did you get the candy?"
*Nonnegotiable rules:* "You can have candy twice a week."
*Negative consequence or penalty for breaking the rule:* No candy for a week.
*Positive consequence or reward for succeeding:* Praise and toys for compliance.
*Negotiable rules:* "Grandpa always brings candy. Let's decide when and how much of it you get to eat. I'll help you store it. You may choose to give some to other people." Child helps identify positive and negative consequences.
*Marshmallowing:* "I can't keep you out of the candy, can I? You're my little sweet tooth."
*Abandonment:* No rules. Sweets always available. Parents don't notice what kids eat and parents eat lots of sweets themselves.

**Bedtime —**
**Child six to twelve years old**
*Rigidity:* "You must be in bed at eight o'clock no matter what day it is or what is going on. No exceptions."
*Criticism:* "You never go to bed when I tell you to. Don't you dare get out of bed and don't turn your light back on."
*Nonnegotiable rules:* Parents will choose a bedtime that allows the child to get enough sleep, so child wakes on her own in time to get ready for school.
*Negative consequence or penalty for breaking the rule:* "If I have to call you in the

morning, you will have to go to bed fifteen minutes earlier that night."
*Positive consequence or reward for succeeding:* "For a week of success, we will do an activity of your choice on Saturday."
*Negotiable rules:* "On weekends and vacation days you can help decide on your bedtime." Child helps identify positive and negative consequences.
*Marshmallowing:* "Try to get to bed earlier tonight. I'll finish your chores for you."
*Abandonment:* Pays zero attention to bedtime or keeps kids up late at the whim of the parent.

---

**Natural and Logical Consequences**

You may be thinking, *How do I decide on appropriate penalties and rewards?* There are two types of consequences that can be used when establishing penalties and rewards. They are natural consequences and logical consequences. It is helpful to know how they differ.

*Natural consequences* happen as a direct result of a behavior. They are either positive or negative. Many times, experiencing the natural results of behavior is the best lesson the child or an adult can have — when he pushes someone and gets pushed back, when she forgets her lunch and goes hungry, when he speeds and gets a ticket, or when she studies and does well on a test. The learning that results is about choice and responsibility.

*Logical consequences* are used as negative consequences when natural ones would be dangerous, too long in coming, or would be a great inconvenience to the rest of the family. Look at what parents said about the differences between logical and natural consequences in the book *Help! for Parents of Teenagers*[1].

- Natural consequences automatically follow a behavior. Logical consequences are related to the behavior and make sense to a person who is thinking clearly about it.
- Failing a course because she doesn't study is a natural consequence. Having to stay home on weeknights to study is a logical consequence of the failure.
- Losing a friend for being rude is natural. Writing a letter

of apology to that friend is logical.

- In making contracts with our kids, we spell out the logical consequences we will impose if the contract is not kept.
- Missing lunch at school because she forgot to take her lunch is logical. Being hungry because she missed lunch is natural.
- Having to walk is the logical result of missing the school bus. Feeling tired is the natural result of walking a long distance to school.
- Taking away television privileges for fighting at school is not logical. Having a problem-solving session with the child and with people at the school or insisting that the school enforce rules about fighting is logical.

Responsible parents do not allow children to make self-destructive or jeopardizing choices. If children do make those choices, the parent does whatever is necessary to help the child back onto a healthier path. Responsible parents do not allow a child to run into the street in order to experience the natural consequence of being hit by a car. Nor does the parent notice a destructive pattern of chemical use, and allow the natural consequence of death without attempting to intervene.

In the next four examples, rewards and consequences have been identified as natural or logical. Notice the differences and think about other possible logical consequences for each.

---

**Time to eat —**
**Child six to twelve years old**

*Rigidity:* "We always eat together at eight, twelve, and six o'clock. No food between meals. If you are not here at mealtime, you don't eat."

*Criticism:* "You forgot to be home in time for dinner again. You'd lose your head if it wasn't fastened on! No dinner for you, stupid!"

*Nonnegotiable rules:* "You must eat some nutritious food at each meal. If you skip a meal you may not eat snacks before the next meal."

*Negative consequence or penalty for breaking the rule:* "If you skip a meal, and eat snacks, I will remove all snacks from the house for one week." (logical)

*Positive consequence or reward for succeeding:* Praise and admiration for good eating habits. Encourage the child to express food preferences and help choose menus. (logical)

*Negotiable rules:* "On Saturdays when we are not having regular meals we will negotiate about eating."

*Marshmallowing:* "I'll fix something for you at any time of day or night."

*Abandonment:* Does not care if child is present at mealtime. Has no regular mealtime.

**Parties — Junior high school age child**

*Rigidity:* "You cannot go to parties at houses, only at school."

*Criticism:* "Those friends of yours are trouble. I bet there will be drugs and who knows what else. I don't trust you. Of course you can't go."

*Nonnegotiable rules:* "You can only go to parties at houses when the parents are home and are supervising the parties. Parents being upstairs is not enough. You are to call us anytime you feel unsafe and we will come and get you."

*Negative consequence or penalty for breaking the rule:* "If you stay at an unsupervised party, I will call the adults before your next party and make sure they will be there supervising. I may also ground you. I may ask for a meeting of the parents of the other kids at the party to discuss some common rules and consequences. (logical) My trust in you will be shaken." (natural)

*Positive consequence or reward for succeeding:* "If you call, I will come for you (logical) and respect you (natural). I will trust you (natural) and extend more privileges to you." (logical)

*Negotiable rules:* "I must know where you are when you are out. Together we will think of ways you can have fun, take care of yourself, and be safe." Child helps set negative and positive consequences.

*Marshmallowing:* "I want you to be popular, so go to all the parties you are invited to. Do you need some new clothes?"

*Abandonment:* "I'm going to a party myself. Do whatever you want."

**Daughter, thirteen, reports that she is being picked on by a boy at the bus stop.**

*Rigidity:* "Hit him!"

*Criticism:* "What did you do this time? You always attract trouble."

*Nonnegotiable rules:* "When you are bullied or someone is being mean to you, think about what you can do to stop it."

*Negative consequence or penalty for breaking the rule:* Reminder of rule. (logical)

*Positive consequence or reward for succeeding:* Child feels better. (natural) Parent offers praise, affirmations, celebration of success. (logical)

*Negotiable rules:* "It is not okay with me that you are picked on. If that happens, we will think about different ways you can deal with the situation. Kids are not for picking on!" Child helps identify rewards for success.

*Marshmallowing:* "Oh, sweetie! Who is it? I'll call his mother."

*Abandonment:* "So?"

**Use of the automobile — New driver, just reached legal driving age and passed licensing examination.**
*Rigidity:* "Don't ask for the car. I'll decide when you need it and when you don't."
*Criticism:* "Take the car? Ha! Are you kidding? I don't want my car wrecked. You would wreck the car for sure."
*Nonnegotiable rules:* "You must observe the traffic laws. For now, you are not to have more than two other kids in the car, and not to go beyond the city limits."
*Negative consequence or penalty for breaking the rule:* No personal use of the car for a week. (logical)

*Positive consequence or reward for succeeding:* More liberal use of the car. (logical)
*Negotiable rules:* "When you have driven with us enough for us to be satisfied with your skill level, then you can drive farther and give more kids rides." Teenager helps identify negative and positive consequences.
*Marshmallowing:* "I know you want the car. I need it too, but I'll take the bus."
*Abandonment:* "Do as you like." Or parent is gone, drunk, preoccupied, or is ignoring or teasing instead of setting limits.

---

### Are There Consequences for Parents?

Parents sometimes ignore that there are also rewards and penalties for them for keeping or not keeping their part of the parenting bargain.

When we first introduce the idea of a contract as a mutual agreement with rewards and penalties for both parents and children, the children may often retort, "Ha! There are no penalties for adults. When grown-ups break contracts with kids they get by with it." After we talk for a while, the kids realize that they do penalize adults. The kids admit, "After that, I don't trust them as much, or I'll take longer to do the work they ask me to do."

Sometimes consequences for adults are as obvious as when a child confronts a parent with, "You didn't do your part." More often the child penalizes the adult with the natural consequence of passive behavior such as ignoring rules, forgetting, sullenness, lack of trust, messiness, tardiness, insolence, failure at school, or flaunting family values.

As parents, it is important for us to keep our part of the contract or own up to breaking it and accept the consequences. We may prefer choosing logical consequences for ourselves rather than accepting the natural consequence. "If I have promised to pick you up at a specific time and I am late, I will do your chores for you," is the offer of a logical consequence.

As you interact with your children, begin to notice when you use the different positions on the Structure and Rules Chart. When you hear yourself using Rigidity, Criticism, Marshmallow, or Abandonment positions, pause to think how you could set limits more clearly by deciding if the situation calls for a Nonnegotiable or a Negotiable rule. Or does the situation call for you to accept the consequences for your behavior in a more responsible way?

## Messages that Support Structure

There are two types of messages that support the development of healthy Structure in people of all ages. One involves *credit and approval for jobs well done.* The other involves the knowledge that when you are doing poorly, someone will care enough to *help you do better.*

Let's take the first message, the one involving credit and approval. Listen to some examples: "I admire how you do that!" "You wrote a great paper." "Wow! Good job!" "I liked the way you combined colors in that painting."

The other message that supports structuring is used to tell someone what they are doing poorly and how they can do better. This one is particularly challenging to give or accept if we have learned to be responsible for other people's feelings. But this message is not about "making people feel bad," it is about caring enough about others to show them how to do better.

The message is most helpful if offered in this way: "Don't do that because. . . do this instead." For example: "Don't use that saw to cut with the grain of the wood. It is for crosscuts. Use the ripping saw instead. I'll show you how." Or, "When you criticize me, I don't like it and I feel mad at you. Tell me what you don't like and what to do instead."

*Any ''stop that'' message that does not also say what to do instead is criticism, not Structure.* The overriding consideration to keep in mind when using this message with children is to deliver it in a steady, clear, and caring way. The words, the voice, and the demeanor must be firm and loving.

Sometimes a child will choose to hear these messages not as Structure, but as criticism. Then he may avoid you, accuse you of "yelling" at him, or do something that lets you suspect he feels ashamed.

When you notice that a child seems to be converting an "I like what you do" or a "You can do better" message into criticism or shame, you can intervene. For example, if he rejects compliments, you can:

- Kindly say: "You need more practice at accepting compliments."
- Ask him to listen for the caring in your compliment as you repeat the message. Use a quiet voice.
- Say: "I'm not sure you heard me. Please listen again. Listen for my love. Listen and believe what I'm saying."
- Give him a very gentle, loving, playful nudge on the arm and say: "I expect you to listen to me."
- Say: "I don't like that you don't accept what I say in the spirit in which I give it."
- Touch the child gently, even shoe to shoe, and repeat the message.

### Toward Structure, Away from Shame and Victim Blame

You may have recognized some of your own childhood experiences in the examples on the chart. Maybe your parents used rigidity, criticism, marshmallowing, or abandonment. If they used lots of these, you may need to grieve not getting the helpful structuring you deserved. You can decide now how to get and begin taking in new Structure messages.

Some of the most powerful negative messages we carry are old criticism or marshmallow messages we heard from adults when we were children. Paying attention to these old messages and voices can make us our own worst enemy. They encourage us to confuse guilt about our behavior with shame about our being. Think about your old messages and notice if you are using old, destructive language when you talk to yourself.

If your parents used marshmallowing, you learned the language of caretaking — those who take care of others' needs at the expense of their own — and you may be neglecting to hold yourself and others accountable in healthy ways now. It is important to notice if you are blaming others when you should be accepting more responsibility for your own attitudes, feelings, and behaviors.

For instance, sometimes people create destructive messages where none were intended; they *convert* Structure messages into criticism or blame. This is the language of shame. People who grew up without enough healthy Structure "blocks" had to use criticism "blocks" instead. These contained a little Structure and a lot of criticism. As these people grew older, they may have decided not to take any more criticism. "I had enough of that as a kid," they say, "I don't need any more. I don't should on myself and I won't let anyone else should on me." They are so accustomed to hearing Structure in a critical tone that when they hear straight Structure, they automatically assume it is critical. They

- reject the Structure because they hear it as critical,
- sabotage the project or activity, or
- blame the sender: start an argument, bad-mouth the sender, or hang on to bad feelings until they have enough piled up to warrant lashing out.

Instead of blaming others, some people raised with criticism, abuse, or neglect, learn to cope by blaming themselves. When these people are given criticism or Structure which they perceive as criticism, they

- feel hurt but comply,
- feel ashamed and comply, or
- run away or forget.

Children who blame themselves and are told to do something, say, "I should have known how to do that.... I should be able to figure everything out on my own.... If I have to be told to do something, it means I am in trouble."

As adults, when a teacher, employer, or mentor tells them they are doing a job poorly or behaving inappropriately, they translate it as, "You bad person! What's wrong with you?"

People who blame themselves for the criticism, marshmal-lowing, abuse, or neglect they receive from others suffer from internalized victim blame.

Victim blame is the process of using words or actions that blame victims for their plights. These are some examples of victim blame:

- Hitting a year-old child for touching things. (It is the job of a child that age to explore everything. Her parents should offer her a safe place and distract her when she approaches something that is unsafe.)
- Calling a two-year-old terrible when he says "no." (It is the job of a two-year-old to practice thinking separately from his parents. His parents could call him "terrific" for practicing saying no because he will need to know how to say no to many things during his life.)

- Making fun of a six-year-old who is afraid to start a new school. (A six-year-old is learning that the world is a big place. Her parents could accept her fear, take her to school to see the place, explain the rules to her, and reassure her.)
- Ridiculing a teenage boy whose voice is changing. (His parents need to find a complimentary way to celebrate the onset of puberty.)
- Touching a child sexually or making suggestive innuendos and then telling her it is because she is flirting or pretty. (Grown-ups are always responsible to offer children and young people only respectful, nurturing interactions.)

When people experience a great deal of victim blame as abused or neglected children, as victims of sexual abuse, as recipients of racial and other prejudices, or as victims of institutionalized violence, such as being spanked at school, beaten by police, or hazed in the Marines, they often internalize the victim blame and blame themselves. Here are some examples of internalized victim blame:

- "Mom would have loved me if I hadn't been such an active kid." (Instead of, "I deserve parents who love and are willing to handle me as I am.")
- "My beauty is a mixed blessing. Because of it, my sister's boyfriend started having intercourse with me when I was eight." (Instead of, "My sister's boyfriend raped me when I was eight.")
- "My spouse wouldn't drink so much if it weren't for me." (Instead of, "My spouse drinks too much.")
- "If I am quiet/good/clean the house/get good grades/make jokes/keep their attention on me, they won't drink." (Instead of, "My parents drink too much and I need help.")
- "If anyone finds out I had sex with my parent they won't like me so I won't tell." (Instead of, "I am the child of a parent who committed incest. I expect you to know this crime is very hard on victims, whatever their age, and I need help and support.")
- "My parent is in jail. I suppose you won't like me." (Instead of, "My parent is in jail. *She* did something wrong. And I expect you to see *me* for myself.")

If we convert "do this" or "you can do better" messages into victim blame and feel ashamed, vulnerable, resist, or want to blame other persons or circumstances when we receive reasonable direction, we can use these cues to decide to believe differently about ourselves. We can learn to hear a "You're doing poorly, here's how to do better" message as helpful. We can practice hearing these messages as support rather than criticism. We can decide to be competent, thriving people instead of victims. Also, we can remember that *we* can decide how we will use the other person's information to improve the way we are behaving or doing a task.

It is true that sometimes other people don't give a "You can do better" message well. They deliver their lines with words or tones that sound critical to us. But even when they really are critical, we can still listen for the helpful part of their message. We can choose to ignore the critical part and not take that in. *We deserve helpful Structure, not criticism.* We can take the part of the message that is helpful and use it to improve our lives and our skills.

### Compliments

Another way we get information about Structure is from compliments — when others tell us we did a good job, finished on time, organized well, or showed creativity.

Compliments are hard for some of us to hear. Some of us learned not to expect praise for a job well done or to be admired for what we did. We may have believed we were supposed to know how to do things perfectly, even if we weren't shown how. Now, when someone makes a positive, congratulatory statement to us, we discount it and stop ourselves from building that healthy Structure into our self-esteem. We may think we must disqualify the compliment or earn it in retrospect. Since we can't accept the compliment as true, we try to make it true by doing something special after the fact.

Instead of throwing away affirming messages from others, learn to let them in. Say, "Thank you," and stop. Breathe deeply and take in the good stuff. If this is hard, do it anyway. As you practice telling your children how impressed, proud, and pleased you are when you see them doing things well, practice telling yourself this also.

### Structure for Adults

Read the examples of healthy nonnegotiable and negotiable rules included in this book over and over and remember that you *deserved* to hear them when you were little and you *can* and should hear and incorporate them now. You can use them with your children and you can offer them internally, to yourself.

As you read the following three examples, think of the messages coming from someone you trust and respect, or as messages we give ourselves. Remember that you are no longer a child but an adult who is in charge of selecting the Structure that works best for you.

---

*Situation:* **A colleague is in trouble with the boss and asks you to lie for her.**

*Rigidity:* "Never tell a lie, no matter what."

*Criticism:* "You're a fool if you do. You let people use you all of the time."

*Nonnegotiable:* "Other people are responsible for their behavior and choices and so are you."

*Negotiable:* "Weigh this request against your own value system. Get more information if you need to."

*Marshmallow:* "Help her out. You don't want to get on her bad side."

*Abandonment:* "Avoid thinking about it."

*Situation:* **Your best friend is telling racist jokes.**

*Rigidity:* "You must always laugh at jokes that a friend tells."

*Criticism:* "He's a bigot and you are dumb for listening."

*Nonnegotiable:* "Telling racist jokes is not okay. Tell your friend to stop."

*Negotiable:* "Consider the most effective response you can think of."

*Marshmallow:* "Your friend doesn't mean any harm. Laugh to make him feel good."

*Abandonment:* "Laugh and forget about it."

*Situation:* **You've been asked to accept a volunteer job on the church fund raising committee and you are already very busy.**

*Rigidity:* "If the church asks, you must do it."

*Criticism:* "You are always so selfish. It wouldn't hurt you to extend yourself a little."

*Nonnegotiable:* "If accepting the job would overextend you physically and emotionally, don't do it."

*Negotiable:* "You can turn down any job that is offered. Think! Do you want to accept it, or fulfill your obligation in another way that suits you better?"

*Marshmallow:* "Go ahead and do it. You can squeeze it into your schedule somewhere. Miss some sleep if you need to."

*Abandonment:* "I don't care what you do."

Consider the positive and negative consequences for keeping and breaking the nonnegotiable and negotiable rules in this set of examples. You may find that sometimes the consequences for keeping the rules are that you will not please others, but you will build your self-esteem and will have a sense of integrity, correctness, and honor. The consequence of breaking the rule is to compromise or abandon yourself and your beliefs to avoid controversy.

### Using Healthy Rules and Boundaries with Other Adults

Use the Structure positions ("Rigidity," "Criticism," "Nonnegotiable," etc.) to identify areas where you are setting healthy boundaries with other adults. Remember that when you take good care of yourself you are more able to take good care of other people. If you don't believe this, think of the times you have neglected yourself and, as a result, others took advantage of you or were angry with you or you were angry with them.

Read the following three examples and decide if you would use one of the four nonsupportive responses in each example. If so, decide if the nonnegotiable and negotiable rules suggested would fit your situation. If not, revise them so you can successfully set boundaries. Look through all of the examples. If some of them seem more difficult than others, skip them until you have studied the easier ones. Remember that the difficult ones may be close to a problem you need to address courageously.

---

*Situation:* **Partner's drinking is interfering with family and job.**
*Rigidity:* "Get out!"
*Criticism:* "You good-for-nothing! What's the matter with you?"
*Nonnegotiable boundary:* "Get help with your problem. I will get help too."
*Negative consequence or penalty for breaking the rule:* "If you do not get help, I will make whatever change I need to make for my own welfare and the welfare of the children, including the possibility of a separation."

*Positive consequence or reward for succeeding:* Praise, admiration, appreciation, relief. A happier family.
*Negotiable boundary:* Continued support of problem drinking is not negotiable.
*Marshmallowing:* (to self) When the stress on the job eases, the need to drink will lessen. I'll continue to make excuses.
*Abandonment:* Observes partner drink destructively without comment.

29

*Situation:* **Spouse is to pay household bills and lets them run overdue.**

*Rigidity:* "You must always pay the bills the day they come in. If you let them go overdue one more time I'll take the household money away from you and I'll make all the household spending decisions."

*Criticism:* "What? Again? You are not fit to be trusted with money!"

*Nonnegotiable personal boundary:* "Our agreement is that I (or we both) put money into the household account on the first of the month and you manage it. I don't want us to spend money on interest so pay the bills on time."

*Negative consequence or penalty for breaking the rule:* Anger and disappointment firmly expressed once. Lessened trust until trust is reestablished by paying on time. Or spouse pays interest from own personal allowance.

*Positive consequence or reward for succeeding:* Praise, affirmations for doing well. Appreciation.

*Negotiable boundary:* "Do you want to review and possibly renegotiate our agreement after we have both calmed down?" Together, plan rewards and negative consequences.

*Marshmallowing:* "Tell me how much money you need." (laughs)

*Abandonment:* "I don't care what you do. You handle all of the money so I don't have to think about it."

*Situation:* **Advice to a friend whose spouse has a drinking problem.**

*Rigidity:* "There's nothing to be done. Drunks are all alike. She'll hit bottom."

*Criticism:* "Why do you tolerate it? She is dumb for drinking and you are just as dumb for putting up with it."

*Nonnegotiable boundary:* "Get outside help for yourself. Until you do, I will not continue to listen to you complain."

*Negative consequence or penalty for breaking the rule:* When friend starts to talk about spouse's drinking, remind friend of nonnegotiable rule and end the conversation or change the subject.

*Positive consequence or reward for succeeding:* Praise, a mutually planned celebration. Support for friend's self-care.

*Negotiable boundary:* "I am willing to support you in finding help. How can I do that?"

*Negative consequences:* If friend does not take action on suggestion for help, move back to nonnegotiable rule above.

*Positive consequence:* Celebrations, continued support, praise.

*Marshmallowing:* "You poor thing. It must be miserable. You can talk to me as often as you need to. Feel free to call anytime."

*Abandonment:* "I have troubles of my own."

**Test Your Knowledge**

Test how well you are identifying the Structure points. For the following examples, after each response, write "Rigidity," "Criticism," "Nonnegotiable," "Negotiable," "Marshmallowing," or "Abandonment" as the Structure point you think fits most closely. Remember that tone of voice, body language, and context can move some responses from one point to another. Compare your answers with the answers of the authors and decide which ones are correct for you.

**Daughter, 16, tells mother about being sexually molested by a friend of the family.**

The mother says:

1. "That's just awful, but I'm sure you will forget about it soon. He's from a good family so we won't tell."

   _____

2. "What did you do to bring it on?" _____
3. "That happened to me too." _____
4. "He must be stopped from molesting you or anyone else. Let's think of all the things we could do and then decide which one to do first." _____
5. "There must be no scandal about our family. Do not mention it again." _____
6. "No one should be sexually abused. I will call a child protection agency. I will see to it that you are safe. We will get this abuse stopped now." _____

*Answers:* (1) Marshmallowing. (2) Criticism. (3) Abandonment. (4) Negotiable. (5) Rigidity. (6) Nonnegotiable.

**My counselor or my support group points out ways that I support addictive behavior in my family. Shall I try to change my behavior?**

1. Each day, I will pick a way I support addictive behavior and hold myself accountable. I will get a friend or counselor to monitor me lovingly, and we'll celebrate my successes. _____
2. I don't want to upset my family or rock the boat.

   _____

3. I can't change. _____

4. I'll listen to the feedback and I agree to look closely at my behavior and what I might want to change. _____

5. I'm too old to change. I hope she gives up her addiction. _____

6. I have botched everything I've tried. I can't do anything right. _____

*Answers:* (1) Nonnegotiable. (2) Marshmallowing. (3) Rigidity. (4) Negotiable. (5) Abandonment. (6) Criticism.

If you identified eleven or twelve of the twelve items correctly, you are superb at recognizing the Structure positions. Nice going if you were correct on nine or ten of the items.

If you labeled seven or eight correctly, keep on practicing; and if you scored six or fewer, don't be discouraged. Honor yourself by rereading the Structure material as many times as you need to and celebrate your willingness to make changes.

### Negotiable Rules — Teaching Children to Think

Negotiable rules are mutually agreed upon; both parents and children offer ideas and make judgments. Sometimes, as parents, we avoid negotiating rules because we believe that to negotiate with kids means to give in or show weakness. Actually, the opposite is true. When we negotiate rules that are appropriate for kids to help decide, we teach our children to think clearly. We show strength in our willingness to hear their needs, to understand their reality, and to rethink our own positions. Negotiation stimulates children to think responsibly and to acquire new information.

Negotiating rules means making contracts. Contracts help parents and children be more clear about who is responsible for what. Sometimes it helps to clarify responsibilities by writing a contract. (See "Using Contracts," Appendix A.)

Topics covered during negotiations include: What? How? When? Where? Who? How much? How long? Then what? Why? Parents ask questions about the child's request because they need information with which to determine the limit or boundary needed for the child's protection and safety.

Notice how the parent questions the child in the following example.

NEGOTIABLE RULE:

Bill, a fifth grader, negotiates with parents before accepting social invitations.

NEGOTIATION:

*Bill:* "Sam has invited me to go to the lake this weekend. Can I go?" (where)

*Parent:* "Well, we aren't doing anything special so tell me what you know about the trip." (what)

*Bill:* "His mom and dad and two other friends are going." (who)

*Parent:* "Which friends? Do I know them?" (who)

*Bill:* "You know Joe but I don't think you know Kelly." (who)

*Parent:* "Yes, I remember Joe. What else can you tell me?"

*Bill:* "We'll leave Friday after school and get back Sunday evening." (when, how long)

*Parent:* "Is there a phone where we could reach you in an emergency?" (how)

*Bill:* "I'll find out."

*Parent:* "Are you all riding in Mr. and Mrs. Albert's car, and do they have seat belts?" (how)

*Bill:* "Yes. And I'll need enough money for food at McDonald's on the way up and back." (how much)

*Parent:* "I see. Will you ask the Alberts how early you'll get home Sunday evening? It's a school night." (how long)

*Bill:* "I'll find out after practice tonight." (when)

*Parent:* "When will you do your weekend chores?" (when)

*Bill:* "I'll ask Lilly to do the sweeping for me and I'll do some Thursday night and maybe you'll help me out if I do extra next week?" (who, what, when)

*Parent:* "Yes, I will. Okay, I think you can go. We'll talk again after you know about the phone and the time you get home. Find out what you'll be doing so we'll know what to pack." (when, what)

Negotiation ends when the parent and child are satisfied or when the parent decides the situation is no longer suitable for negotiation. For instance, in the previous example, if Bill would not be home before eleven o'clock on Sunday night, his parent would have said that he could not go. Parents are responsible for a child's health. Bill's parent believes that a fifth grader needs to be at home and in bed well before eleven o'clock on a school night. When the parents set this type of boundary, they establish a nonnegotiable rule that has penalties and rewards.

Negotiating these many factors teaches children how to think, encourages them to be responsible, and sets the expectation that they will use their energies and power in positive ways. Also, parents can remember that as children grow up and have less physical touch from their parents, one way they get attention and make contact is by challenging, arguing, and hassling. The process of negotiating gives kids, who like to connect with their parents by hassling, a constructive ground on which to do that.

During the negotiating process, the child learns he can count on his parents. He also learns important lessons in life: *I win sometimes, you win sometimes, we both win sometimes; so I can feel good about winning. I can learn to handle disappointment. I don't have to always win. I can learn skills for cooperation.*

If both parent and child feel as if they've lost, it's time for parents to take another look at the household rules and at their ability to negotiate clear contracts and enforce rules with love and Structure, not punishment and criticism.

### How Many Negotiable Rules?

As children grow older it is important to increase the number of negotiable rules, making some of the formerly nonnegotiable ones negotiable. Consider the skill and maturity level of the child when deciding to do this.

Following are seven examples of areas suitable for negotiation. Either a parent or a child can initiate the negotiations.

### Money
Family rule: *We are all to be suitably dressed, and we have this much money in the family budget for clothes.*
*Parent opens negotiation:* "You have this many dollars for your share of the clothing money this fall. The things you want cost more than this amount. Let's talk about what we can do."
*Child opens negotiation:* "All of the kids in my class wear designer jeans. I want some too."

### Grades
Family rule: *If you let your grades slip, you must spend more time studying.*
*Parent opens negotiation:* "It's two weeks since your last report

card. How are you doing on bringing up your grades?"
*Child opens negotiation:* "I've been studying for two hours in my room each school night since the last report card. I'm doing better now and I want to cut down on the study time."

## Convenience

*Family rule: Seventeen-year-old Rod drives younger brother Jason to practice.*
*Rod opens negotiation:* "I'm going to the Speech Regionals next weekend. I'd like to be excused from taking Jason to Little League practice. Can someone else take him?"
*Parent opens negotiation:* "Rod, Mrs. Smith is wondering if you can take Christopher to practice too. Do you think that you could handle both boys?"

## Chores

*Family rule: Everyone helps with chores.*
*Parent opens negotiation:* "Here are the chores that have to be done this weekend. Let's decide together who does which one when."
*Child opens negotiation:* "I'm bored with my chore. I'd rather do something that's fun."

## Skill Level

*Family rule: Jason can bike within a half-mile radius of home, crossing the highway only at the stoplight.*
*Child opens negotiation:* "I know how to ride my bike really well and I follow the safety rules. Can I bike to Lake Independence with my friends on Saturday?"
*Parent opens negotiation:* "Jason, I see that you are handling your bike really well. Want to take a bike trip with me Saturday to see if you are ready for a larger territory?"

## Maturity Level

*Family rule: As children grow, they learn new skills and get new responsibilities and privileges.*
*Child opens negotiation:* "I think I'm old enough to shop for Mom's birthday present alone."
*Parent opens negotiation:* "If you feel ready to shop for Mom's birthday present alone, you could do it today while I'm at the hardware store."

**Social Manners**
Family rule: *Social manners and customs should be appropriate to the situation.* Teenage son wants to wear his earring to Grandma's reception.
*Parent opens negotiation:* "We are going to see Grandma. I know that you like wearing your earring, but I'm afraid Grandma and her friends will misunderstand the statement you are making."
*Son opens negotiation:* "I suppose you'll ask me not to wear my earring when we see Gram. I wish she'd get used to it."

Use this chart to list some of the negotiable rules you have or wish you had in your family.

**Money:**

**Grades:**

**Convenience:**

**Chores:**

**Skill Level:**

**Maturity Level:**

**Social Manners:**

**Other:**

**Other:**

# CHAPTER 2

# *Using Rules as Structure Tools*

Once we decide to replace Rigidity, Criticism, Marshmallowing, and Abandonment with Negotiable and Nonnegotiable rules, we need to think about:

- What are rules and why are they important?
- What are nonnegotiable rules?
- Which rules are nonnegotiable?
- What are negotiable rules?
- How do we negotiate rules?
- How do we keep rules current?
- How do we set consequences?
- What if parents disagree about rules?
- How do we enforce rules?

## What Rules Are and Why They Are Important

A rule is a boundary or limit that sets a standard and has consequences for compliance and for noncompliance. Rules are established to hold people, ourselves included, accountable.

One way parents set solid boundaries is by making and enforcing rules appropriate to a child's age and abilities. When rules are humane and made for the safety and protection of the child, children learn that they deserve to be safe and that their parents love them. And they learn even more. They learn that they deserve to feel successful; to be successful; to be proud of accomplishments; and to live richly, mindful of themselves and others.

Clear, positive rules help children develop a personal framework to use in keeping themselves physically and psychologically safe from harm and for getting their needs met. Children who acquire helpful rules and boundaries from their parents avoid unsafe situations. They have a low tolerance for the invasion of their personal boundaries by people who want to use or take advantage of them. They are good at inviting positive people and experiences into their lives and at keeping negative experiences and people out.

Rules help us teach children about safety and limits. Also, in the process of teaching rules, parents give children a supply of helpful information about themselves and their environment that they can store for later use. Before children can make sense of a rule and internalize it they need adequate information from parents to realize that a particular rule is for their welfare.

## Nonnegotiable Rules: Commands and Demands

Let's review the difference between Negotiable and Nonnegotiable rules before we explore when to use them. Think of Nonnegotiable rules as commands or demands, and Negotiable rules as applying to any situation where you negotiate on what to do.

Nonnegotiable rules are boundaries or standards of behavior that we insist upon. They are commands and demands. Some of us have difficulty in making and enforcing Nonnegotiable rules because we are reluctant to think of them as commands or demands. So we tell children how we feel rather than what to do. (Listed in Appendix A in the section "Asking for Change" are eleven ways to give children information about their behavior. Six of the ways express commands and demands; five offer support, encouragement, and challenge.)

If we believe nice adults don't give commands or demand appropriate behavior from others, we may pretend that we have made a contract with other people about their behavior. To make a contract is to make a voluntary agreement between two or more people. This is what we do when we *negotiate* rules with children. There are many things in our lives that must be done; some are voluntary and some are not. If I tell someone to take out the garbage, I have given a command. I have made a one-way decision, I have not asked for a volunteer nor have I negotiated a contract.

Commands are an important part of parenting. Three year olds are comforted by commands such as "Don't play in the street. Play in the yard." Even though they may hassle and object loudly, older children and adults sense the protection in commands that are appropriate to their age and safety. A "Be home at ten o'clock, it's a school night" is an appropriate limit for a fourteen-year-old. A "Don't drink and drive" to another adult tells her you care about her and demand she make responsible decisions. And yes, even a "Take the garbage out" lets children know that adults know how and when to be in charge.

Nonnegotiable rules appropriate to a child's age give safety and protection and let the child know he is a capable, and important, contributing member of the family. Sometimes children hassle about rules because the rules are oppressive. But they also hassle to test their power, to test their parents' determination, and to make contact. Parents can use this kind of hassling creatively as an enjoyable way to connect with a child. (See "Creative Hassling," Appendix A.)

When demands are not abusive or used with rigidity, they teach the value and importance of being healthy, interactive members and law-abiding citizens.

Each family has to decide which rules are nonnegotiable and which are negotiable. Making those decisions and knowing when to change Nonnegotiable rules to Negotiable rules as the children grow, is part of the art of parenting.

Here is a guide to areas where *Nonnegotiable* rules are suitable with one possible example for each.

**Health:** "You will stay in bed when you have a fever."
**Safety:** "You may not drive if you have been drinking."
**Legality:** "You may not drive without a valid license."
**Ethics:** "I will not call your boss and lie for you."
**Religion:** "You will attend services with the family until you are fourteen."
**Family Traditions:** "We all go to Grandma's house on her birthday and on Christmas Eve as long as she is well enough to have us."
**Parental Preference:** "You may not turn the volume high on your music when I am in the house."
**Community Customs:** "This is a quiet neighborhood. If it is a special occasion and you let the neighbors know ahead of time, you may have a party and loud music that lasts till midnight once or twice a year."

Some of these examples may not fit for your family. Remember that nonnegotiable rules differ from family to family. Children can learn that families do things differently and that their family is unique.

Use the following chart to list examples of the *Nonnegotiable* Rules that you have or wish you had in your family. You may think of additional categories.

**Health:**

**Safety:**

**Legality:**

**Ethics:**

**Religion:**

**Family Traditions:**

**Parental Preference:**

**Community Customs:**

**Other:**

**Other:**

In order to decide which rules are to be negotiable and which are to be nonnegotiable, parents need to be clear and straight about their own values and about what is safe and what is unsafe, what is helpful and what is not helpful. Those of us who grew up without getting the help we needed to assess danger need to consult with other people who are already good at it. Check out your reality in regard to safety with as many other people as you need to. Do not discount your needs or your child's needs for safety and protection.

To help all family members be clear about family rules, post the important ones, both the negotiable and nonnegotiable rules. (See "Sample Rules Charts," Appendix A.)

## Keeping Rules Current

Sometimes after a child has been observing a rule or keeping a contract for a while, she starts breaking it. As long as a youngster sees a rule as reasonable and workable for her, she is apt to comply. But when she begins to feel the rule is too restrictive or does not account for her increased abilities to be responsible for herself, she may resist or defy the rule by breaking it or forgetting it. When children do this frequently, it's time to examine the rule. Perhaps the rule is no longer appropriate. (Otherwise she may be signaling you about some other distress in her life.)

When your child breaks the same nonnegotiable rule or a contract two or three times, say, "It's time to discuss this situation. We will look for new information — information we didn't consider when we first made this rule. Let's meet tomorrow." Remember that updating or negotiating a rule is best done when people are calm rather than in the heat of disagreement or resentment.

As parents, you may decide to reassert the rule and stiffen the consequences, particularly if the safety of your child is involved. Or you may decide that a rule you negotiated giving the child more responsibility needs to be made nonnegotiable for a while or renegotiated, since the child has shown an unwillingness to keep the contract.

*Probably the most useful information a parent can have in deciding which rules should be nonnegotiable and which should be negotiable is what development tasks are appropriate for what age. Parents need to know what to expect from children of various ages and stages of development.* (See Chapter 7)

## Setting Consequences

Appropriate consequences, both rewards and penalties, provide children with important Structure and contribute to their self-esteem. A reward that a child feels she has earned is an esteem builder. When a penalty that she knows she deserves is delivered without rancor or blame, she can decide how to feel about it. She may decide to feel awful about herself for a while, or she may feel stronger for having learned from her mistake and made amends. She can also feel confident that her parents are dependable and really will follow through.

If parents neglect to set reasonable consequences, children learn other lessons. They may learn to pay attention to rules only when there is an abusive authority to fear. Or they may decide that rules are not important because they are not enforced. If parents neglect to recognize, admire, and celebrate compliance with rules, children may learn that they have to break rules to get attention. If parents neglect to hold themselves accountable, children may learn that accountability is only for youngsters.

Parents who need to think more about appropriate consequences can refer back to Natural and Logical Consequences, page 19.

## When Parents Disagree about Rules

When parents disagree about a rule, they may decide, if it is a minor rule, to have Mom's rule and Dad's rule and let the children learn about handling differences. For example, if the kids miss the bus when they are with Dad, he takes them to school because school is important to him. If they miss the bus when they are with Mom, they walk to school or stay home and study all day because learning responsibility is important to her.

If, however, parents disagree on an important rule, they will have to come to agreement, even if this means "fighting it out." In John Bradshaw's *The Family*,[2] he lists ten rules for fair fighting. You may want to pursue them at length.

Here is a shortened version of them.

1. Be assertive, not aggressive.
2. Stay in the now.
3. Avoid lecture; stay with concrete, specific behavioral detail
4. Use "I" messages; avoid judgments.
5. Be rigorously honest.
6. Don't argue over details.
7. Don't assign blame.
8. Use active listening.
9. Fight about one thing at a time.
10. Go for a solution, not for being right, and hang in there unless you are being abused.

## Enforcing the Rules

Remember that all rules, whether nonnegotiated or negotiated, only work if they are enforced. So do that. Reward children when they obey a rule and penalize them when they do not.

Actually, all behaviors have consequences, positive and negative. If we as parents forget to provide positive consequences — that is, rewards, celebrations, expressions of trust, thanks, or approval when children perform well — we neglect a powerful method of encouraging children to build their own positive Structure. Sometimes parents inadvertently punish good behavior by assigning another chore as soon as the first one is completed. Unless this is part of the contract for the day, with rewards at the end, what this teaches the child is not to finish unless he wants more work.

So give children the positive consequences they deserve and teach them to do the same for you.

Also deliver the negatives, the penalties, when they are needed. Children deserve to know ahead of time what the consequences will be for not complying with a demand, and they need to experience situations where demands or commands are consistently enforced. This clarity and consistency also help provide the positive Structure building blocks children need. Children will not necessarily like having the penalties enforced, but that's okay. Do it anyway.

Janet approached her daughter, Heather, who had been restricted to the house for the evening. Evenly and lovingly, Janet said, "I'm sorry you have to stay home tonight. Remember, it's part of my job as a parent. . ."

"To have me hate you?" Heather interrupted.

"No, to set up and carry through consequences," her mother responded in a matter-of-fact, nonthreatening voice.

An important thing for parents to remember is to set penalties that discomfort the child and that the parent is willing to deliver. How many parents have "grounded" a child for a week only to find themselves miserable with the arrangement?

And how many parents have threatened a consequence they did not want or intend to carry out only to find that the child still disobeyed, forcing the parents to do something they really didn't want to do?

When this happens, or when a child has been deliberately marching around the edge of his parents' patience, parents can breathe deeply, sit or stand tall, and remind themselves that they do love this child. The question, "What do you need and what do I need?" calmly asked, will often break the escalation and open negotiation for a peaceful settlement.

When parents' anger has built beyond the point where it

helps them enforce rules fairly, they will need to discharge their anger before they discipline the children. Some parents can do this by counting to ten; some by promising themselves they can scream later, while alone in the car. Many parents need a physical release, so they hit a pillow to keep from striking a child. Using a Fuss Box is one way to move anger's energy and begin solving the problem at hand. (See "The Fuss Box," Appendix A.)

Later, parents can look at their Structure to see if it needs refurbishing. Remember, *punishment* is treatment that is harsh or unrelated to a child's behavior. It is what we do when we feel powerless or when we haven't carried through on consequences and penalties that were effective. This may be a clue that we need new rules or more skills in order to continue teaching our children.

Parents can care for themselves by cultivating a network of supportive adults to call for help. This network may consist of family, friends, a parenting class, neighbors, or a Parents Anonymous group. All parents need support and they often need it most when they have to enforce rules.

### Protecting Children from Adults

Sometimes parents need to provide safety for children by providing Structure for other adults. There are many easy ways to do this, as when we fire a careless baby-sitter or keep children away from a punitive adult. The following four Structure examples represent areas that are often more challenging for parents to handle: ridicule by a family member, compulsive caretaking, religious rigidity, and incest.

Read each one and think about the possible effect on the children and the adults if each position were used. Remember that as we offer better Structure for our children, we also develop stronger Structure in ourselves.

**Example One**

Problem: Mom hears Dad laugh and say to three year old: "Your ears stick out. You look like Dumbo the Elephant!"

Mom says to Dad:

*Rigidity:* "If you ever say that again, the boy and I are leaving."

*Criticism:* "Henry, you are always calling names. You're the dumbo."

*Nonnegotiable rule:* "Ridicule is damaging. Stop ridiculing our son or I will have to think of what action to take."

*Negotiable rule:* "It is not okay to talk to our son like that. Is there some way I can help you stop ridiculing and start affirming?"

*Marshmallowing:* "Henry, you are such a tease!"

*Abandonment:* Doesn't say anything to father or son.

**Example Two**

Problem: I saw my spouse touch our child in a sexually stimulating way. I say to spouse:

*Rigidity:* "I will never let you see the child again as long as you live."

*Criticism:* "You pervert! You never do anything decent."

*Nonnegotiable rule:* "Either you leave temporarily now, or I will leave with the child now. You cannot be with any of our children until and unless experts decide it's safe for all of us to be together again."

*Negotiable rule:* None. Sexual touching of a child by any adult is not negotiable.

*Marshmallowing:* "Honey, when you do that, it makes me feel anxious."

*Abandonment:* Pretends not to notice.

**Example Three**

Problem: Mother is depressed and threatening suicide.

Dad says to child, age nine:

*Rigidity:* "What you want is not important. You must take care of your mother now."

*Criticism:* "Now what did you do to make her feel so bad? Don't do anything that will worry her."

*Nonnegotiable rule:* "It is not your job to keep your mother from hurting herself. I will see that she gets the help she needs." Finds adequate help for the mother and care for child and for himself.

*Negotiable rule:* Getting help for Mom and child is not negotiable.

*Marshmallowing:* "I'm sorry you have to ignore your friends to keep an eye on your mother. If we give her lots of attention, she'll be better soon."

*Abandonment:* Dad spends time with a girlfriend or at work and ignores child.

**Example Four**

Problem: My religious group has the correct rule and practice for every situation. They believe in disciplining children by using fear and the paddle. These are messages to myself.

*Rigidity:* "I will adhere to the teachings of my church and my religion even if I have to abuse my children to do so."

*Criticism:* "If I don't follow the rules, I am a bad person."

*Nonnegotiable rule:* "Beatings harm children and scaring kids makes them fearful, not strong. I will learn how to structure without abuse or intimidation."

*Negotiable rule:* "I will learn how to set rules and when to listen and negotiate with my children."

*Marshmallowing:* "I'm uneasy with what our leader says about punishing children, but the leader must be right."

*Abandonment:* "I follow my church's teachings, and I ignore my children's feelings, needs, and reactions."

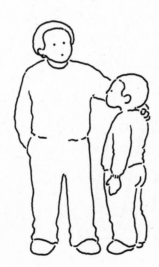

**Martin's Story**

Martin was abused as a child. The Structure in his home was critical and loose. The rules changed from day to day. When he broke the rule of the day, he got harsh punishment. He learned to stay low and not make waves. Since Martin did not like the harsh parenting he received, he decided to parent differently. He gave in to his children in order to please them. He sacrificed himself for them and didn't make and enforce rules because he was afraid if he did they wouldn't love him. He continued his marshmallow parenting and became a martyr. He left his children, as he was in his childhood, without the protection, security, and freedom that only firm, consistent rules can give.

When his children began to have troubles at school and with friends, Martin decided to do some things differently. In his parent support group he asked for help. He was tired of feeling powerless and ineffective. With the help of the group members he identified some affirmations and new rules that would help him care for himself and his children. Martin was "growing up again." His messages, which he repeated daily and gradually came to believe, were: *I am important. I deserve love and respect. I can learn to be a firm, loving, respectful parent.* Martin accepted that it was his job as a parent to set the rules, that he would keep getting support, and that he would stop trying to please the kids when they disagreed with him.

Here are the twelve aspects of Structure that Martin's group studied:

1. All behavior has consequences — positive or negative.
2. Penalties and rewards must be related to behavior to be effective. It's the parent's job to decide if natural or logical consequences are more appropriate penalties.
3. Children must know the consequences of breaking rules ahead of time and are often good at helping to decide on those consequences.
4. Setting, negotiating, and enforcing rules is an act of love and is the job of the parent. Whether the kids thank, fuss, hassle, pout, or threaten to leave, is up to them. Parents may decide to hassle but they must provide Structure. (See "Creative Hassling," Appendix A.)

5. Discipline is the process of teaching children skills and attitudes for taking care of themselves and others, based on self-esteem. Fear, shame, and ridicule have no place in that teaching. Parents who use shame and ridicule because they need to control their children find that it works because it brings children to their knees. What parents don't realize is how hard it is for children who have been ridiculed to stand up again.

6. Punishment is hurtful stuff parents do when they feel scared, vindictive, or tired, and it indicates that they need new Structure, stronger boundaries, and new rules to protect and care for themselves and their children. Penalties are effective for children only if they motivate healthy growth in the child.

7. Few rules are better than many. Martin started with thirty-seven, cut back to twenty, and finally got to six.

8. It is a good idea to write the rules and to post them. (See "Sample Rules Charts," Appendix A.)

9. It is okay, important, and essential to get help when you don't know what to do or if you have tried all the things you know and the problem remains unsolved. (See "How to Find a Support Group Or a Therapist," Appendix B.)

10. It is okay to make mistakes and to keep working at correcting them until you do correct them.

11. It is okay to apologize, to say, "I'm sorry I did that and I won't do it again."

12. It is important to be true to the best that is in you.

Listen to Martin now:

"Nat is just beginning to use the car and has permission to take it on short runs around town. I pay for the gas but he is not to let the gas level fall below a quarter of a tank. If I go to use the car after he has used it and find less than a quarter of a tank, he doesn't use it again until he pays for a tank of gas out of his own pocket. This is nonnegotiable. I do negotiate with him about when he will use the car, where he is going, for how long, with whom, and what he'll be doing."

Martin had a lot of support and he borrowed ways to structure from other people who already did it well. As he got better at setting positive rules for his son, he realized it was getting easier to set healthy boundaries for himself.

You, like Martin, may realize that your parents used the ways described in this chapter as not-so-helpful. If this is true, you now have the challenge of changing the parenting legacy you inherited. You can. You can learn helpful Structure for yourself and you can teach it to your children.

## Structure With Love

Structure is believable and acceptable to a child when the child feels loved. Structure without love and Nurture is harsh and constitutes only half of what children need. In the next chapter we address the other half of the life-giving formula — Nurture.

# SECTION II

# NURTURE

## The Gentle Side of Care

*Great love can both take hold and let go.*

**— O.R. Orage**

# CHAPTER 3

# Nurture
## Acts of Unconditional Love

In the last chapter we focused on Structure. Now we'll look at Nurture, the other half of the parenting and self-care issue. Structure is about doing; Nurture is about *being*. Structure is the skin and bones of life; Nurture is the soft tissue that fleshes out the skin and helps the bones move freely.

In this chapter, we will consider:

- Nurture — what it is and why it is important.
- Care and support — expressions of unconditional love.
- The Nurture Chart — ways children get love and attention.
- More about care and support — some distinctions.
- Your new parenting skills.
- How to help children accept love.

*Nurture is all the ways we give love to ourselves and others.* Nurture is important because it helps people of all ages thrive and develop. It offers us the hope, joy, and self-confidence to be ourselves, to be successful. We store it, droplet by droplet as the basis of our self-esteem. Nurture encourages us to hear and believe positive Structure. When we feel loved we are not apt to hear, as criticism or shaming, the "Do this" or "Do this differently" of Structure messages. When we know we are lovable we feel worthy and expect to ask for and get Structure. Nurture helps us develop our uniqueness and our skills.

Young children need to be nurtured, to be touched, noticed, and cared for. Nurture provides them with the attention and contact they need in order for them to decide to stay alive and to live fully. Indeed, Nurture is so essential that children who

53

are not noticed and are touched very little fail to thrive, and can die.

*Attention and contact help children live.* Of course, some forms of attention and contact are much healthier than others. Children who are hit, treated harshly, or violated sexually, *are* touched and noticed. They often, but not always, manage to grow up. In the absence of positive touch and care, those children "make do" with the harsh contact available to them. They live, but often without hope, joy, confidence, and competence.

People whose childhood was filled with unconditional love, with Nurture, pass it along naturally to their children. The rest of us, although we may be determined to give our children the good parenting we did not have, don't know how. Learning new ways takes thought, determination, time, and sometimes discomfort. There is, however, joy in this process. It comes as we watch our children thrive and as we learn to nurture ourselves and become truly more confident and hopeful.

## Care and Support — Expressions of Unconditional Love

We will begin our discussion of love by looking at what children need. You can use this chapter to help you nurture your own children and to think about ways you were nurtured. After we have considered the ways children get or don't get loving care, we will consider what adults, whose lives lacked or lack healthy care, can do to heal themselves. Perhaps the child in you needs extra care and support.

True nurturing comes in two forms, assertive care and supportive care. *Assertive care* means that the caregiver notices, understands, and responds to the cues and requests of the child. The caregiver determines what the child needs, and responds to those needs in a loving, trustworthy, and reliable way. *Supportive care* is the act of offering care at appropriate times. The child is free to accept or reject this care.

The foundation of both assertive care and supportive care is unconditional love. Its expressions are many.

- "I love you and care for you because you are here."
- "I love you because you are you."
- "You deserve love. No strings attached."
- "I love who you are."
- "I love and care for you willingly."
- "I love you."
- "I'm so glad to know you."

- "I'm glad you're my son/daughter."

Unconditional love has no price tag. It uses no yardstick to measure worth. It is given freely, as often and as much as needed. Children who receive this kind of care thrive, master their developmental tasks in a natural way, and are free to be fully alive. It is this opportunity to thrive that may be the greatest gift parents can give.

## IDENTIFYING POSITIVE AND NEGATIVE PARENTING

We will use a Nurture and Care Chart on pages 58–59 to examine positive and negative ways parents offer contact and attention. The positive ways, Assertive Care and Supportive Care, are in the center of the chart. The negative ways of offering or withholding contact we call Abuse, Conditional Care, Indulgence, and Neglect. On the chart, the six points are arranged in order of *hardness:* Abuse, Conditional Care, Assertive Care, Supportive Care, Indulgence, and Neglect. Abuse, on the one end, is a harsh way of making contact. On the other end of the scale, neglect gives almost no contact or care.

As you start to use the chart, please remember the following:

- Become familiar with each position on the chart before you start evaluating how you are parenting. Remember, you probably use more than one position and your children get the composite of all the positions the adults in their lives use.
- Each position on the chart represents a pattern of parent behaviors and child responses typical of that particular position. Nevertheless, since each child's interpretations and decisions are uniquely his own, a particular child may not "fit" these examples.
- The information on the chart is organized so you can trace a nurturing position vertically to examine your understanding of that position. You may also look across the chart to compare how common underlying messages, responses, and decisions differ.

Abuse and Neglect are at opposite ends of the chart, but, although abuse has the most contact and neglect the least, the effects of these two are very similar. The *Abuse* position is  characterized by painful, invasive behavior toward the child. Included here are humiliation, shaking, burning, hitting, sexual touch or innuendo, laughing at pain, threats of harm, scolding for being in pain, and ridicule. Parenting from this position offers harsh "drops" of contact for the child to incorporate. Some forms of abuse are piled up by the child as single "drops." Other types of abuse such as beating, kidnapping, molestation, or incest, even if they happen only once, will be incorporated by the child as a monstrous cluster of "drops." That one experience usually gives rise to decisions that have a deep-rooted, long-term, traumatic effect on the development of the personality. This happens unless these decisions are revisited, usually in conjunction with therapy.

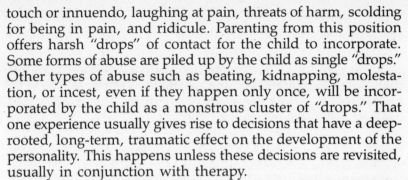

The *Neglect* position describes parenting that ignores the child's needs because the parent is "too busy," or physically or emotionally absent. This includes ignoring the child's need for care and contact, and ignoring pain. Single experiences of Neglect also may be laid down as individual drops or as traumatic clusters.

Both abuse and neglect deny a child's needs and interfere with his development in profound ways. Children who grow up with abuse or neglect are often abusive as adults, or they shut down aspects of their lives, or both. Alice Miller describes this process in detail in her books, *The Drama of the Gifted Child*, and *Thou Shalt Not Be Aware: Society's Betrayal of the Child*.[1]

*Conditional Care* and *Indulgence*, while not as harsh as Abuse and Neglect, also deny a child's needs. Children who receive conditional care are cared for only when they earn care. "I will care for you if . . ." Their *being* and *doing* get bound together. They are expected to turn their being into doing and give up their need for unconditional love. When people equate who they are with what they do, their ability to thrive is thwarted by a burden of constantly proving themselves worthy and never being able to do so. Frequently, the result is a feeling of shame.

*Indulgence* is smothering. Indulgent parents shower a child with more attention or material things than she needs and before she even asks. Sometimes, she is expected to enjoy things her parents "know she would like," things they would have liked, or things that push her to grow up too fast.[2] Her needs and wishes are anticipated. As an infant she is fed before she indicates she is hungry. She may be treated like a doll. She is not allowed to become responsible for identifying her needs and learning to meet them herself.

Her ability to thrive is thwarted by her lack of opportunity to strive. She may like the indulgence when she is young, but after she moves into a world that expects competence, her feelings may change from satisfaction to confusion, resentment, and shame.

*Assertive Care* and *Supportive Care*, the two positions in the center of the chart represent positive, responsible nurturing appropriate to the child's age and development. *Assertive Care* means meeting a child's needs directly. It is what the parent does for the child. *Supportive Care* is the loving presence of the parent who offers help.

# Nurture and Care Chart

## Ways Children Get Love and Attention

Joy, hope, self-confidence, and self-esteem grow from care and support. Despair, joylessness, and loneliness flow from abuse, conditional care, indulgence, and neglect.

## Situation: School age child has a badly scraped arm

| Abuse  | Conditional Care  | Assertive Care ◯ |
|---|---|---|
| *Characteristics:* | | |
| Abuse is relating to a child by assault, by physical or psychological invasion, by direct or indirect "don't be" messages. Abuse negates the child's needs. | Parents who use conditional care connect with the child by the use of threats and conditions. The care the parent gives the child is based on the parent's needs and expectations, not on the child's needs. | Assertive Care is comforting and loving. It is freely given, it is helpful to the child, responsive to the child's needs, and appropriate to the circumstance. |
| *Example:* | | |
| Parent does not care for wounds. Says, "Stop sniffling or I'll give you something to cry about." Parent yells at or shakes the child. | Parent says: "Stop crying or I won't bandage your arm." | Parent gives loving care and a hug. Cleans and dresses the wound. Says, "Your arm is scraped! I'm sorry." |
| *Children May Hear the Following Underlying Messages:* | | |
| You don't count. Your needs don't count. You are not lovable. You don't deserve to exist. To get what you need you must expect pain. | I matter and you don't. Your needs and feelings don't count. You can have care as long as you earn it. Don't believe you are lovable; you have to earn love. | I love you and you are lovable. You are important. Your needs are important. I care for you willingly. |
| *Common Responses of Children:* | | |
| Pain in the heart, as well as pain in the scraped arm. Fear, terror, rage, withdrawal, loneliness, despair, shame. | Pain in the heart, as well as pain in the scraped arm. Fear, terror, anger, mistrust of own perceptions, shame, feeling of inadequacy. | Pain in the arm and warmth in the heart. Feels comforted, accepted, important, satisfied, relieved, secure, safe, loved. |
| *Decisions Often Made By Children:* | | |
| I am not powerful. I deserve to die, or the reverse, I will live in spite of them. It's my fault, or the reverse, I'll blame everything on others. I'll be good, or the reverse, I'll be bad. Big people get to abuse, or I can abuse those smaller than me, or I will never abuse. I won't feel or have needs. Love does not exist. I am alone; I keep emotional distance from, and don't trust, others. I blame or strike or leave first. | I am what I do. I must strive to please. Big people get what they want. I can never do enough. I must be perfect. I don't deserve love. There is a scarcity of love. I must be strong. Love obligates me and is costly. I don't trust. I do keep emotional distance, run away, or blame others. | I am important. I deserve care. It's okay to ask for what I need. I belong here. I am loved. Others can be trusted and relied upon. I can know what I need. It's okay to be dependent at times. |

| Supportive Care ○ | Indulgence ᓂ | Neglect ⬚ |
|---|---|---|
| Nurturing support offers help, comfort, and love. It encourages the child to think and to do what she is capable of doing for herself. | Indulgence is a sticky, patronizing kind of love. It promotes continuing dependence on the parents and teaches the child *not* to think for himself and not to be responsible for self or to others. | Neglect is passive abuse. It is lack of attention emotionally or physically, by parents who are unavailable or who ignore the needs of the child. These parents may be "there, but not there." |
| (Parent has already taught child how to clean a scrape.) Says in a concerned and loving tone, "I see you've scraped your arm. Does it hurt? Do you want to take care of it yourself or would you like some help from me?" Offers a hug. | Parent rushes to child. Says, "Oh, look at your arm, you poor thing. That really stings! I'll bandage it. Go and lie down in front of the television and I'll do your chores for you." | Parent ignores the scrape. Says, "Don't bother me." |
| I love you, you are lovable. You are capable. I am willing to care for you. Ask for what you need. Your welfare is important to me. I am separate from you. I trust you to think and make judgments in your own best interests. | Don't grow up. Don't be who you are (capable). My needs are more important than yours (or) your needs are more important than mine. We can't both get our needs met at the same time. | You are not important. Your needs are not important. You do not deserve to exist. Expect to suffer to get what you need. Be confused about reality. |
| Pain in the arm and a heart filled with confidence. Child feels cared for, comforted, challenged, secure, and trustworthy. | Pain in the arm and uncertainty in the heart. Self-centered satisfaction, temporary comfort. Later on: helplessness, confusion, obligation, resentment, defensiveness, and shame. | Pain in the heart, as well as pain in the scraped arm. Feelings of abandonment, fear, shame, rage, hopelessness, helplessness, abject disappointment. |
| I am loved. I can know what I need. I am capable. I can be powerful. I am not alone. It's okay to ask for help. I am both separate and connected. I can decide when to be dependent and when to be independent. | I am not capable. I don't have to be competent. I don't have to know what I need, think, or feel. *Other people are obligated to take care of me.* I don't have to grow up. I must be loyal to my indulging parent. To get my needs met, I manipulate or play a victim role. It's okay to be self-centered. Later on: be wary and don't trust. | I don't really know who I am or what's right. I am not important or powerful. I am not lovable. I die or survive alone. It isn't possible or safe to get close, to trust or to ask for help. I do not deserve help. What I do doesn't count if someone has to help me. Life is hard. |

## More About Care and Support — Some Distinctions

Both care and support are provided willingly with no strings attached. They differ in subtle and important ways. Care is a loving response or loving intrusion. Support is an offering, lovingly given.

Infants require care. They signal their need by crying or fussing. Baby Sally cries and Dad offers her a bottle. She refuses it and Dad tries gentle rocking. She fusses for a bit, then settles into his arms, satisfied. He has made loving responses and given Supportive Care. When the furnace breaks down and Dad puts warmer clothes on Sally before she starts to cry from the cold, Dad has made a loving intrusion. He has given Assertive Care.

As children grow older they need more support and less intrusion, but even big, competent kids appreciate assertive care now and then. Judy's teenage son had been making his own lunches. One morning, when he overslept, a school project due that day broke when he packed it. Judy made his lunch for him, handed it to him with a smile, and said, "I made lunch for you today. I hope the rest of your day is better." Her loving intrusion was welcomed by her son. He felt cared for and affirmed.

Although support is needed less often than care by young children, it is helpful to them because it gets them started on making decisions and it encourages them to think about how they feel and what they need. Little Sally, now a toddler who has been busy exploring the objects on the end table, starts to fuss and looks tired. Dad says, "Sally, I have a rocking chair and a big hug for you. Do you want to rock?" Sally gets to choose whether to be rocked, fuss some more, or wander off to another activity. If her fussing increases, Dad will switch from support to assertive care.

When parents take good care of their children, the children grow up knowing how to take good care of themselves. As children are able to be more responsible for meeting their own needs, parents decrease the amount of assertive care they provide and increase the amount of support they offer. The growing relationship between parents and adult children becomes primarily one of support going in both directions.

Besides offering care and support to our children, it is fun to indulge them at times. But it is important to examine how often and why we do this. If we try to nurture the "child inside" us by indulging our "outside children" it may feel good to us, but it is a message to our children that they count only as a reflection of us. When we learn to meet our own needs directly we no longer want to overindulge our children.

Some parents put the children first in order to play the martyr. Such parents do not truly value themselves and are seeking validation from their children. Hence, they do not want to deny the children's wishes or risk their wrath. Martyr parents, who indulge, often raise children who are selfish and unappreciative of others. Children with parents who undervalue themselves will not learn to value the parents, themselves, or others. Lacking a model for true self-worth, a child tries to construct a sense of herself by copying her parent's martyrdom, or, seeing the futility of that, tries its opposite: running over the needs of others to get what she wants for herself.

We all might play the one who indulges or the martyr at times. But we need to counter these tendencies by learning to truly value ourselves and others. Use the following Nurture examples to evaluate the parenting you are doing.

You can assess and improve your skill at offering care and support to children by thinking about the following examples. Decide if the care and support suggestions would be helpful if your current family were in that situation. If not, rewrite the care or support messages and behaviors in a way that would be more appropriate for your family. Remember to base them on unconditional love.

**Example One**

**Situation:** One-year-old child puts everything in his mouth.

The parent:

*Abuse:* Screams at child and hits objects out of his mouth.

*Conditional Care:* Frowns, says, "I don't love you when you do that. Be a good boy and stop."

*Assertive Care:* Takes all hazardous or breakable objects out of rooms where child plays. Admires child's ability to explore.

*Supportive Care:* Offers a wide variety of objects that are safe for child to mouth.

*Indulgence:* Lets child ruin things because "he wants to chew on everything."

*Neglect:* Doesn't notice child tasting colored tissue paper, cigarette butts, aspirin, dishwasher soap.

**Example Two**

**Situation:** Three-year-old starts to cross street alone.

The parent:

*Abuse:* Spanks.

*Conditional Care:* Pulls the child back and says, "I won't love you if you don't obey me."

*Assertive Care:* Calls to child and dashes after her. Enforces nonnegotiable rules about crossing alone.

*Supportive Care:* Acknowledges child's wish to cross, while reminding her that she will learn how to cross alone when she is older.

*Indulgence:* Gives child permission to cross alone before she is able to judge speed and distance of cars.

*Neglect:* Looks the other way.

**Example Three**

**Situation:** Four-year-old boy plays dress up in women's clothes.

The parent:

*Abuse:* Says, "You're a little queer!" Snatches jewelry off the child and/or beats him.

*Conditional Care:* Says, "I love you only when you are acting tough like a real boy should."

*Assertive Care:* Says lovingly, "I see you like playing dress-up." Offers hug.

*Supportive Care:* Provides a variety of dress-up costumes.

*Indulgence:* Buys six fancy costumes that reflect "real boy" activities such as a cowboy suit, pirate outfit, Superman costume.

*Neglect:* Provides no props for fantasy play.

**Example Four**
**Situation:** Seven-year-old child is feeling sad about being excluded by friends.

The parent:
*Abuse:* Says, "I don't blame them. I wouldn't want to play with a crybaby like you." Hits child on upper arm or twists his ear.
*Conditional Care:* Sighs, says, "I'd always hoped that you would be popular."
*Assertive Care:* Says, "I love you and I think you are wonderful. I'm sorry they left you out. What are some other things you can do today?"
*Supportive Care:* Says, "I remember a time when I was your age and was sad about being left out. It felt icky. Remember that I'm on your team. Anything you want from me?"
*Indulgence:* Says, "I'll get you some new toys and then they will want to play with you."
*Neglect:* Doesn't notice or says it doesn't matter.

**Example Five**
**Situation:** Ten-year-old wants to learn to play a French horn.

The parent:
*Abuse:* Says, "You want to play a horn?" in a ridiculing way. Laughs at child. Makes a paper cone and sings loudly in child's ear.
*Conditional Care:* No praise, focuses on mistakes or urges sports instead. Says, "I don't have the money for a horn because you need better skis."
*Assertive Care:* Says, "On Friday we'll go to the music store and find out about renting a horn and getting a good teacher."

*Supportive Care:* Says, "I think you will do great. I hope there's a recital soon so I can come listen."
*Indulgence:* "Here, I got you a trumpet. It's a very good one. It'll be easier for you to carry than a French horn."
*Neglect:* Ignores child's request, or promises to get an instrument and forgets.

**Example Six**
**Situation:** Family is moving to different town and ten-year-old child does not want to move.

The parent:
*Abuse:* Says, "Don't be a crybaby. If you're going to whine, I'll give you something to cry about."
*Conditional Care:* Says, "I have a lot to do so be cheerful and help me pack."
*Assertive Care:* Sees child's tears. Holds the child. Comforts the child. Gives child a book about a child's experience with moving and talks with the child about it. (Ann Banks and Nancy Evans' book, *Goodbye, House: A Kid's Guide to Moving* is a good children's book about moving.)
*Supportive Care:* Says, "Leaving the place you live and your friends is tough. Want to plan some special ways to say good-bye to your friends?" Adults do some good-bye ritual about leaving the home and invite the child to join them.
*Indulgence:* Says, "I feel sorry for you. I moved twice when I was your age. You can have your choice of the bedrooms and all new furniture in your new room."
*Neglect:* Fails to notice child's distress.

63

**Example Seven**

**Situation:** Onset of puberty.

The parent:

*Abuse:* Teases about acne, budding breasts, or voice changes. Touches child in sexual manner.

*Conditional Care:* Says, "I see you are starting to mature. I'll buy you a bra, but I hate to see you growing up."

*Assertive Care:* With a loving voice, says, "I notice your body is changing. You are entering adolescence and becoming more grown up. That's a wonderful, important change. I love who you are." Continues to offer to touch child in nurturing, nonsexual way that is acceptable to the child.

*Supportive Care:* Says, "This is an important milestone! How would you like the family to celebrate? Would you like us to choose a gift for you?"

*Indulgence:* Says, "I see you are starting to mature. I'm glad! Now you can have boy-girl parties. Let's plan one for this Friday."

*Neglect:* Doesn't notice or withholds touch. Some parents confuse nurturing touch and affectionate touch with sex and stop touching children of the opposite sex at this time when most kids feel insecure and need the reassurance of our continued safe, parental touch.

**Example Eight**

**Situation:** Teen is surrounded by pressure to use alcohol.

The parent:

*Abuse:* Regularly searches teen's personal belongings, listens in on phone conversations. Grounds or beats him after hearing that there was beer at a party he attended.

*Conditional Care:* Says, "I love you as long as you don't drink." Or, "You'll be the death of me if you drink."

*Assertive Care:* Does not offer liquor to teenagers. Offers car when appropriate so teen doesn't have to ride with peers who are drinking. Affirms love for and importance of the teen on ongoing basis.

*Supportive Care:* Does not drink or uses in moderation, never to intoxication. Indicates understanding of peer pressure to use. Asks how to be of help. Encourages teen to develop a variety of skills and awareness for coping with pressure. Celebrates successes.

*Indulgence:* Offers to buy liquor for teen.

*Neglect:* Drinks to excess, is emotionally and/or physically absent; doesn't notice kid is drunk.

**Example Nine**

**Situation:** Teenager acts severely depressed.

The parent:

*Abuse:* Says, "Don't mope around here. You have nothing to be depressed about."

*Conditional Care:* Says, "Come back when you are cheerful." Or, "You think *you're* depressed!"

*Assertive Care:* Takes child to a professional for assessment and gets therapy if needed. Makes necessary changes in the family system.

*Supportive Care:* (Getting help is not optional. Support is not enough.)

*Indulgence:* Commiserates. Lets child stay alone in room. Buys expensive presents. Says how bad life is.

*Neglect:* Doesn't notice or says, "I see you are growing up. I hope that you make it."

**Example Ten**
**Situation:** Child is disabled.
 The parent:
*Abuse:* Calls child gimp, cripple, peg-leg, half-wit, et cetera. Cares for child roughly.
*Conditional Care:* Withholds comfort when child is suffering. Praises when child denies grief and sadness.
*Assertive Care:* Teaches child to cope. Validates child's feelings.
*Supportive Care:* Offers a variety of opportunities for child to grow and thrive.
*Indulgence:* Does not expect child to be responsible for his own feelings or behavior. Does things for the child that child is able to do for self.
*Neglect:* Does not provide care, support, or protection for child.

**Example Eleven**
**Situation:** Teenage daughter was raped.
 The parent:
*Abuse:* Beats her or blames her for attracting the rapist.
*Conditional Care:* Says, "You can't expect people to respect you now. Let's not tell anybody about this."
*Assertive Care:* Gets professional help for whole family. Uses all resources, personal and external, to help daughter, self, and family heal.
*Supportive Care:* Is willing to listen or to talk with her. Offers to be available. Does whatever is necessary to heal self. Family does something in an effort to prevent rape. Daughter can help do that if she chooses to.
*Indulgence:* Sends child on a trip to Europe to get her mind off it.
*Neglect:* Doesn't notice. Since daughter is used to neglect, she does not tell.

 You can write Nurture Charts like these for yourself as often as you need to. Teach your children to recognize the responses as a tool for evaluating what kind of Nurture they are getting outside of their family. Teach them to expect care and support and to recognize and reject abuse, conditional love, indulgence, and neglect.

### Helping Children Accept Love

If you think your child is rejecting or converting nurturing messages to criticism, or if the child is not accepting the love you offer or is feeling ashamed, ask yourself:

*Is the child being abused by someone else? By someone who is cruel and mean? Or by someone who does not understand his developmental needs and is interfering with them?* If this is true, protect your child and get help. Dr. Christine Ternand has described this kind of child abuse in her *Help for Parents* books.

Has your own parenting been uneven? If so, tell your child that you have been inconsistent and are going to change, and do change! Also try the following:

- Report to your child that you are not sure he heard your nurturing message. Ask your child to listen as you say it again. Do not invite a response.
- Touch him gently and repeat your nurturing message directly and softly.
- Tell him you think your nurturing message wasn't heard in the way you meant it. Say you would like to try again. Express the message in a different way. Don't expect a response right away.
- Say the message to yourself. Does it sound nurturing to you? If not, try to restate it in a nurturing way.
- Tell him you are making changes in the ways you express nurturing. If he is old enough, ask how you could say it better.
- Be sensitive to the expressions of caring that each child seems to prefer. Some like to hear it, some to see it, and some to feel it.
- Ask your child to tell you what kind of loving he likes you to give him.
- Point out to him ways that you are accepting love for yourself.
- Point out examples of other people, children or adults, accepting love.

# CHAPTER 4

# Nurturing Other Adults and Ourselves

Adults need Nurture too. The art of nurturing adults consists of an elegant balance — being sensitive about when to offer assertive care and when to offer support. Not too little, not too much. If we don't know how to offer much of either, we can practice and learn. If we offer too much, we are called patronizers, enablers, codependents, or benevolent dictators. If we are good at offering care and support to others, we watch for clues and listen for requests. We need to offer what other people really need, or ask them what they need instead of giving them what we need to give them.

## Assertive and Supportive Care

When do we give adults assertive care? When they are ill, stressed, lost, tired, in danger, hurt, wounded, or frail. Or when they are parents of infants or of newly adopted children. Or if we have an ongoing contract that need not be negotiated daily; for example, I wash your car, you wash my clothes. When people are grieving a loss, they need others to care for them. We may send flowers, drop a note, bring chicken soup, or extend an invitation to a movie. As in all cases where nurturing is appropriate, offering any kind of sexual invitation is not. Often, the most powerful thing we can do is listen. Doug Manning calls it the "laying on of ears."*

While *assertive care* means the caregiver decides what someone needs and provides it, *supportive care* is help that is offered. It may be accepted, refused, or negotiated.

---

* Thanks to Doug Manning for coining this phrase.

Think about these responses to Lynn's offers:

*Offer is accepted*

To a friend experiencing the death of a parent, Lynn says, "I'm sorry about your mom's death. I'd like to help. If you have people flying in for the memorial service I will be happy to make airport runs." Her friend says "thanks," and gives her flight times.

*Offer is refused*

Lynn notices her friend's distress. She asks, "Are you okay? Do you want to talk?"

Her friend replies, "I'm fine," and Lynn says, "Okay, if you want to talk later, let me know."

Her friend has decided not to accept Lynn's offer to talk, but the door is left open if the friend changes her mind.

*Offer is negotiated*

There are times that the help Lynn offers is not what the other person needs. "I'm willing to bring dinner to your house tonight."

"Thanks for the offer. Actually, what I need more than dinner is someone to drive the kids to their lessons this evening. Would that work out for you?"

Lynn checks her schedule and says yes, she can, or sorry, she can't.

Support is characterized by respect. Each person recognizes the other as responsible and each retains a sense of personal power and integrity.

The ability to offer both assertive care and support to other adults springs from a willingness to extend unconditional love that rests firmly on our knowing who we are and what our needs are. Confronting alcoholism is assertive care. Offering encouragement when a friend with a drinking problem seeks help is support. Taking a hot meal to a family with a new infant is assertive care. Offering to baby-sit is support. Giving a surprise birthday party is assertive care. Offering to plan a celebration is support.

**Practicing Assertive Care and Supportive Care for Adults, Others, and Ourselves**

Once you have thought more about your ability to offer care and support, look at the following examples of nurturing that we offer to other adults and to ourselves. Practice discriminating between the positions. Notice when you use positions you want to change and when you use positions you want to keep. *Directions:* Note the Structure positions of Abuse, Conditional Care, Assertive Care, Supportive Care, Indulgence, and Neglect in Examples One and Two. Then, in Examples Three and Four, write in the space provided which structure position best describes the response. If the examples of Assertive Care and Supportive Care don't fit for your circumstances, rewrite them.

---

**Example One**
**Situation:** Husband to wife about who cares for the children.
   The husband:
*Abuse:* Hits or ridicules wife if she asks for help.
*Conditional Care:* Says, "I'll help with the kids when you earn more money than I do."
*Assertive Care:* Says, "Children need care from Dads." Participates in all aspects of child care.
*Supportive Care:* Negotiates with wife about child care. Praises the quality of her care and his care in front of the children.
*Indulgence:* Gives expensive presents instead of helping.
*Neglect:* Works long hours, travels, spends long hours at bars, sports, or civic organizations, comes home late and leaves early.

**Example Two**
**Situation:** Parent to self, "The children's needs come first, then my spouse's, then mine."
   The parent:
*Abuse:* "I'll work as long as I need to in order to provide what my spouse and children want." Works self into illness.
*Conditional Care:* "I'm not a worthwhile person unless I sacrifice for my family."
*Assertive Care:* "I recognize my needs and get them met and help meet the needs of others. All of our needs are important. We work together to get them met."
*Supportive Care:* Parent seeks membership in an appropriate support group.
*Indulgence:* Shops, works, eats, takes pills, or drinks compulsively to ease the stress.
*Neglect:* Continues to act on the old belief.

### Example Three

**Situation:** Partner is addicted.
The addicted person's partner:

1. Excuses partner to children.

2. "Here is where you can get help."

3. "I am getting help for me and the kids. I want you to come with us."

4. Ignores partner's addiction or furthers own addictions.

5. "I will love you when you shape up."

6. Alternates criticism and cold silence.

*Answers:* (1) Indulgence. (2) Supportive Care. (3) Assertive Care. (4) Neglect. (5) Conditional Care. (6) Abuse.

### Example Four

**Situation:** Parent to self, "If I stop keeping up appearances and covering for other family members' unhealthy behaviors, I will have to take care of myself directly and I don't know how to do that."
The parent:

1. Continues the cover-up.

2. "I will focus even more attention on looking good."

3. "I will find a number of people who will support me, so I have several choices."

4. "I am going to see a counselor or therapist and face whatever I have been avoiding in myself."

5. Becomes chronically ill with a stress-related condition.

6. "I'm okay only as long as I'm taking care of others."

*Answers:* (1) Neglect. (2) Indulgence. (3) Supportive Care. (4) Assertive Care. (5) Abuse. (6) Conditional Care.

## Nurturing Ourselves: Personal Rules for Love

If you have difficulty extending both assertive care and support to yourself or accepting it from others, pause now to think about why it is difficult.

Care and support are based on unconditional love. If, as children, we didn't feel loved unconditionally, it may be hard to recognize and accept unconditional love when others offer it to us. If our being loved hinged on how we were useful to our families, we may hold our breath and wait for the other shoe to drop when someone says "I love you." We wonder, *What will I have to do to deserve this?* or *What is this going to cost me?*

If we had to accept long ago that adult needs came ahead of ours, we questioned love and support to ensure our survival. Now we will have to learn to believe in unconditional love and that may take awhile. But we can do it and the better we learn to accept unconditional love for ourselves, the better we will be able to offer it to our children.

## Sex and Nurturing

Each person has favorite experiences and environments that feel nurturing: a walk along the ocean, candlelight, or an exhilarating day of skiing. Since touching and warm, responsive connections with others are such a big part of how Nurture is given and received, many adults have assumed, because of how they grew up, that they must accept or seek sexual touch in order to be nurtured. Sexual activity can be nurturing in the context of a loving relationship, but substituting sexual contact for nurturing leads to all sorts of problems, from personal feelings of hollowness to the destructiveness of incest. It is never okay for anyone in a position of trust to misuse that trust in a sexually exploitative way.

There are many ways adults meet their needs for physical Nurture. Here are a few:

- getting therapeutic massage,
- asking for hugs from friends,
- fostering nourishing relationships with people who love and accept them for who they are, and
- caring for their bodies in a loving way by eating and exercising wisely.

People who use sex in an addictive way need to find a therapist who is skilled, caring, and supportive.

### Choosing to be Lovable

"I am loved, I am lovable, I am loving." These are the un-conditional love decisions. Here are some personal rules that flow from these decisions:

- I accept love freely.
- There is an infinite supply of love.
- I give love freely.
- I surround myself with loving people.
- I protect myself from unloving people.

If we didn't choose these rules as children, if we received uneven parenting, we decided on some other rules that made sense at that time. But those rules keep love away. They reflect our "giving up on love" or our "longing for love."

Look at the old situations, and look at the decisions that some people made and the new rules they have chosen for themselves. We can borrow ideas from them to help us grow up again.

*Alice:* "They said they loved me so I don't examine what they did. I just passed this kind of love on to my children, but I still feel hollow."

*New rule:* I am lovable. I examine my legacy and am doing my healing. I am learning about joy and finding it for myself.

*Devon:* "They didn't love me but I pretend they loved me. I can't stand for me or anyone else to know they didn't so I'll act as if they did or I'll act as if I don't care."

*New rule:* I am lovable and I care about being loved and I attract loving people into my life now.

*Bart:* "They never told me that I did well, that they loved me, or that I was important to them, so I don't tell anyone I love them now. I'm afraid they'll think they're better than me and will leave me."

*New rule:* I affirm myself and accept affirmations from others. I tell others how much I appreciate them, admire them, love them.

*Frank:* "They never told me they loved me so I decided to get love from others. I will do anything for anyone who will say, 'I love you.' "

*New rule:* I am lovable and I deserve love. I am lovable just the way I am, and I don't deny my needs or values to please others.

*Candy:* "They tried hard to buy my love so I didn't trust their love or tell them I loved them. Now I fear that if I tell others how much I love them, they will no longer need me."

*New rule:* I love you and want you to love me and I tell you that.

*Henry:* "They abandoned me so I decided that I don't deserve love. If you love me I am afraid you will leave me, so either I will force you to leave me, or I will leave you."

*New rule:* I will accept your love and do the healing I need to do to be able to stick around.

*Ed:* "I felt ashamed because I didn't feel loved. Now I try to earn your love by anticipating your wants and needs. If you have to ask me to do something, I feel like a failure for not having noticed your need. If you tell me that you love me, I have to figure out something to do to deserve it."

*New rule:* I accept your love freely. I expect you to ask for what you need.

*George:* "They were impoverished, emotionally and economically, so I decided I wasn't lovable and that I needed to earn whatever love I would get."

*New rule:* Real love is free! I can accept it but I can't buy it and I don't need to make trades for it.

*Kate:* "I felt ignored so I connected any way I could. I got in fights or I settled for sex instead of love."

*New rule:* I find positive ways to get attention. I know the difference between sex and nurturing. Now sex enhances love; it doesn't replace it.

*Marty:* "They gave me everything, did everything for me. I loved it! I also loved them. I assumed the world owed me. I hit the world outside of my family unprepared to fail in all of the incredible ways that people fail, so I blamed others."

*New rule:* I am responsible for my own needs. I accept help from others, and appreciate it. The universe does not revolve around me; I am part of it. I am important and other people are important.

These new rules make fine daily affirmations if we have freely chosen them and desire to incorporate them into our lives. In *Daily Affirmations for Adult Children of Alcoholics,*[3] Rokelle Lerner says, "Affirmations are positive powerful statements concerning the ways in which we desire to think, feel, and behave."

You may want to make your own new rules and affirmations as Kate and the others did or you may prefer to use the ones at the end of the book. (See "Developmental Affirmations," Appendix B.)

## Recovery from Indulgence

When people who have been abused, criticized, or loved conditionally recognize the harm done to them and decide to recover, they can find support, recognition, and help. But, people who were indulged often find it difficult to recognize the debilitating nature of their experience; they recognize it later, and it's especially hard for them to find recognition and support.

People who were indulged say, "My parents gave me everything I wanted. They really loved me! How can I call that bad?" When indulged people do begin to recognize that they were cheated it is usually difficult for them to get encouragement and help from others. Tell another adult how you were abused or always had to prove yourself and you will get sympathy. Tell another adult you were indulged and the response is often jealousy or criticism for being spoiled. People are encouraged not to recognize the damage of indulgence, and often make scornful remarks such as "Tough — I wish I'd had some of that." But recognize it we must or we stay stuck in the pain of being only partly grown up, bound by the sweet, sticky ropes left from our indulged childhood.[4]

## Making New Rules

Now think about your situation and the old lifesaving decisions and rules that you made about unconditional love. If some of them are outdated, outworn, or confusing, see them for what they are. When you recognize a decision or rule that now works against you, use that as a signal to stop neglecting yourself or defending your parents and make some new rules that make sense to you now — as an adult and as a parent. The rules can be a part of your healing, growing process.

It is time to look at what really happened. Grieve what you didn't get that you needed and what you did get that hurt you. Your parents may not have had the Nurture they needed and they may not have been able to give it to you, but the truth is, you have never been unlovable, even if you felt unloved. You deserve to do whatever you need to do to grow up again and feel lovable.

After growing up again, Devon said, "Now I am free to feel loved. I don't have to pretend I don't care anymore because I don't have to protect my parents anymore. For the first time

I believe they did love me and in some ways they did the best they could to show me."

Alice said, "I believed they loved me. They told me that. But I had big empty places in me because they neglected me. After I learned to recognize the neglect, I came to accept the love they did give and stopped neglecting myself. Now it is my job to not pass the neglect on to my kids."

*Whether our parents loved us or whether they didn't is no longer the question. Now the issue is — do we love ourselves and do we accept love from everyone who is willing to give it?*

## Accepting Love from Others

As we change any confusing rules we may have about deserving love and being lovable, we will be able to drop the "don't trust" rules that we use to filter out love from others.

Those of us who grew up needing to earn love from our parents became suspicious when it was offered to us by others. We passed love through a carefully constructed filter in our heads, a filter we built because we decided that unconditional love didn't exist. At least not for us.

Now, when we hear "I love you," we ask ourselves, *What does this person want from me?* We meet loving messages with the suspicion that the terms of that love are not on the table. We even convert the love offered to us into criticism or feel ashamed because we are not really good enough to merit it.

When someone offers us support, those of us with highly developed filters are likely to decline the offer. Instead of welcoming aid and checking to see if it is freely given, we reject it. We automatically say, "I'm fine, thanks," or "I'll be all right," or "I don't need any help."

Very serious business! When we throw away nurturing we filter out the very love we long for. This love is the foundation of our self-esteem.

Some of us decided to cope with being unloved and feeling ashamed by being "perfect," being "good," being "right," or being "better." This makes our self-esteem competitive and bases it on the performance of others instead of belief in our inherent capableness and lovableness.

Until we believe and accept straightforward, clean, nurturing love, we rob ourselves of our birthright — to be loved and to believe that we are lovable.

If you are tempted to ignore your new rules about accepting love, or if you convert a nurturing message into a shaming one, do this instead:

- tell yourself to let the message in and notice how it feels,
- ask the sender to repeat the message, and listen carefully,
- say, "Thank you," and
- then ask yourself if this person is trustworthy or if his love has a price tag. If it does, take in the love if you want it but protect yourself from the price.

Remember, we all deserve love; we all deserve to grow up again. When we recognize the importance of Structure and accept our longing for love, why do we continue to keep ourselves from getting and giving those life-sustaining supports? Sometimes we simply need to learn and apply new skills. Usually, if we keep ourselves from "the good stuff in life" we are using denial. The process that supports denial is called *discounting* and we will pursue that in the next section.

## SECTION III

# DENIAL

## The Glue that Keeps Us Stuck

*god save the children*
*trapped in the game*
*living in fear*
*hiding the pain*
*battered by devils*
*screaming in vain*
*feeling the wrath*
*then doing the same*

— **Steve Lynch in**
*The Carleton Voice*
**Volume 50 no. 4**
**Summer, 1985**

# CHAPTER 5

# How To Replace Discounting with Empowering

"Yes, my work does keep me from being with my family, but I am not a compulsive worker. I just find my job interesting and my contribution is essential right now."

"My son has been given three citations for driving while intoxicated, but he really wasn't. He doesn't have an alcohol problem. He drinks socially, but he doesn't drink any more than his friends. Kids will be kids."

"My family has so many things going on that I am too tired and I don't have the time or energy to stay with a fitness program."

These are some of the many faces of denial.

Once a person has made a conclusion about life, especially if that conclusion was made early and under duress, she tends to defend it. Often, old decisions, once made, were put outside of our awareness, where they are followed automatically and not thoughtfully. When behaviors resulting from those decisions lose their usefulness or become downright harmful, she may still maintain a strong position in defense of those old behaviors and decisions. That position is called *denial*. The process of maintaining denial is one of discounting.

In this chapter we'll cover these questions:

- What is discounting?
- What do people discount?
- Can people stop discounting?
- How do people discount?
- What are the four levels of discounting?
- What are ways to change discounting to empowering?

## What Is Discounting?

Discounting is making something more, less, or different than it really is. Discounting is the thought process that maintains a position of lack of responsibility for responding appropriately to a current reality by reacting in a way that attempts to alter the reality to make it fit some previous decision or perception. By discounting, people can redefine a problem, situation, or need, so they believe they don't have to do anything about it.

That perceived lack of ability to do something or understand what is going on is usually based on some old personal decision about lack of power. By discounting, we keep ourselves from acting responsibly. We keep ourselves powerless.

Power is the ability to recognize what we and other people need and to take action on that information. Power misused is exploitative. Positive power is action taken to care for our own needs and the needs of others. But, for some of us, at an early age, it was not safe to act in a way that looked powerful or wise to be honest about what we saw in our families. It was safer to accept the big people's definition of the world, to let them tell us what to say, what to think, even how to feel. Perhaps the family had some secret that children had to deny, even to themselves. So we learned to give away our power by discounting.

Probably all people use denial at times and do some discounting out of habit to protect old perceptions. Some discounts have only small negative effects, but some are deeply serious. Since when we discount we may not be aware we are doing it, we can use the information in this chapter to help us get a clearer picture of what discounting is and to recognize our own habits of discounting. If we find areas where we are discounting, we can decide what changes we want to make to improve the ways we care for ourselves and the ways we parent.

## What Do People Discount?

People discount themselves, other people, and situations. Look at the following ways John discounts and the decisions and beliefs that the discounting protects:

*Self discount:*       "I can't do anything about this situation." (Old decision — "I'm not important or powerful.")

*Discount of others:*    "No point in telling her. She will never change." (Old decision — "She is rigid.")

*Discount of situation:*    "I see the lightning, but it won't strike here. I'll finish my golf game." (Old belief — "It will never happen to me.")

Notice that when a person discounts the situation or other people, he also discounts himself. If John took action he might have to recognize that he *is* important. If he told her and she changed, he would have to update his old opinions about her. If he came off the golf course, he would be protecting himself and admitting that he is mortal.

When the decisions, attitudes, and behaviors that maintain them are deeply embedded in John's past, he discounts without thinking and can be totally unaware of his denial.

### Can People Stop Discounting?

If our habits of denial are longstanding, can we change our discounting behavior? Yes, we can change a bit at a time by deliberately becoming aware of our behaviors. We can think about them. We can gather information by asking other people about their feelings and thoughts about situations. We can deliberately contract with ourselves to pay thoughtful, loving attention to evaluating and making changes in one piece of discounting behavior at a time. It is helpful to put aside any tendencies of self-blame and look upon discounts with an *Oh shucks — well, here is something I can change and I will*, attitude.

Here are seven steps you can use to become aware of discounting behaviors and to replace discounting with empowering, responsible thinking and behavior.

1. Choose a recent situation that disturbed you, but that you did nothing about.
2. Ask yourself what you discounted. What information or feeling did you ignore? What did you not attend to or value? Yourself, others, the situation? Remember that doing nothing is, in fact, doing something. When we do nothing we cast a powerful, apathetic vote that says, "I take the action of ignoring or denying."
3. Brainstorm four or five things you could have done instead. Remember, ideas collected by brainstorming don't have to be sensible. Generate lots of ideas; don't evaluate them until later.

81

4. Predict the probable outcome of each of these actions and decide for each if it would likely have made the situation better.

5. Select the action you plan to use the next time you are in the same situation.

6. Think about how often you discount. How often do you ignore things or fail to think things through because you feel powerless or not responsible? Compare that to how often you choose to ignore or remain silent because you chose that from options as the most powerful way you could help the situation.

7. Choose a new decision that will support your new plan of action, such as, "I am powerful and responsible."

Here is how Virginia went through the seven steps.

*1. Choose a situation*

I was in the grocery store when I observed a mother spanking her two-year-old and then glaring at her baby and threatening, "You keep your mouth shut or you will both go to the car!" Later, as I left the store, I noticed the two children alone in a closed car, screaming. It was a hot day. I did nothing.

*2. Ask yourself what you discounted*

Self: I discounted myself by thinking, *They are not my kids so I'm not responsible and I wouldn't know what to do.*

Other: I discounted the mother by assuming she would verbally attack me if I spoke to her, and I discounted the needs of the children by telling myself that *babies are tough.*

Situation: I discounted the situation by ignoring the fact that closed cars can be heat traps and that I know of instances where children have died in closed automobiles on a hot day.

I did nothing when I could have done something.

*3. Brainstorm*

What could I have done?

A. I could have told the store manager.

B. I could have offered to take care of the children for a half hour.

C. I could have asked the mother if there was some way I could help. "Excuse me, but I remember when my children were little and I needed to get my shopping done. I have some extra time right now. Is there some way I can help you?"

D. I could have given the mother the name and address

of a nearby drop-in center that provides child care for shoppers.

E.   I could have called a child protection agency.
F.   I could have told the police officer who was having lunch across the street at McDonald's.
G.   I could have told the mother, "You stop this — you are abusing your children. You are not a good mother."

### 4. Predict the probable outcome

Working backward through my list, I decided: Forget G. Blaming seldom helps. F — probably would have been successful and it would have been easy to do. E — a good bet, but might have taken them awhile to get there. D — maybe. C — could work, but I was too scared to try that. B — wouldn't have worked because I didn't have the extra half hour. A — possible.

### 5. Select action to use in future

If this happens again, I'll try telling the police. If they won't come and help the children, I'll call a child protection agency.

### 6. How often do I discount in similar situations?

I often ignore how adults treat children. Yet I believe that adults should protect children. Next time I'll brainstorm options. I'll ignore only if I have decided that is the most effective thing to do, not because I am acting powerless.

### 7. Choose a new decision

Adults should protect children and that's what I'll do.

If you recognized some of yourself in Virginia's story, accept that information without blame or shame. We all learned to discount because we needed to. Don't be hard on yourself, that only keeps you stuck. Remember that sometime in the past, when we felt confused or were in pain, we learned to deny and discount by pretending things didn't matter. But, in the long run, they do matter and we pay a price for ignoring what is really going on.

## How Do People Discount?

In order to discount, to distort or ignore information, problems, or options, we use grandiose thinking. We make something "grandly larger" or "grandly smaller" than it really is to justify our denial. We maximize or minimize by holding attitudes that imply "always," "never," "forever," "told you a thousand times," or "not really important."

Whenever we use grandiosity to discount, we are attempting to avoid responsibility. We are trying to shift it to others. In *Power and Innocence: A Search for the Sources of Violence*, Rollo May defines power as the ability to keep what we want to keep and change what we want to change.[1] When we discount, we neglect to take good care of ourselves and we prevent ourselves from taking good care of our children. We give up our power.

## What Are the Four Levels of Discounting?

We can find out more about how we discount by looking at the methods people use to discount. We'll refer to these as levels of discounting. They are described in the book *Cathexis Reader*,[2] by Jacqui Lee Schiff and others.

*Level 1:* Discount the *existence* of the situation, problem, or person. "That's no problem."

*Level 2:* Discount the *severity* of the problem. "That's no biggie."

*Level 3:* Discount the *solvability* of the problem. "You can't fight City Hall."

*Level 4:* Discount your *personal power* to solve problems. "Nothing I can do about that," or "Their needs are important; mine are not."

While discounting at any level denies the importance of the situation, self, and others, it may help to think of each level as having a special focus. First and second level discounts are ways of denying the situation. Third level discounts primarily deny the ability of others and self to find options. Fourth level ones deny the self, one's own needs, and one's own power to take effective action.

When we do not deny, when we take full account of the situation, others, and self, we respond in an empowering way for ourselves and others, a way that gives and accepts full respect and responsibility.

Look at the following three events with examples of all four discounting levels. At the end of each event is a possible response that does not discount, but empowers, and validates respect for self and others.

If you recognize your own behavior in some of the discounting, make a note of it and go on. If you need help stopping critical voices in your head, read *Taming Your Gremlin: A Guide to Enjoying Yourself* by Richard D. Carson. You can decide later how much you want or need to change.

**Family gathers before the funeral of a grandparent.**

*Level 1:* "Hi folks. What's new?" (No problem)
*Level 2:* "You can't expect people to live forever." (Not serious)
*Level 3:* "Nobody can help anyone else with their grieving. It's a lonely road." (No solution)
*Level 4:* "I ought to be able to help my family through this but I just don't know how." (No personal power)
*Empowering:* "I'm glad I'm here with you. I feel bad about Grandpa and it's hard for me to believe he's dead. How do you feel?"

**Pet dies and family member says to child:**

*Level 1:* "Don't carry on so — it wasn't a person you know." (No problem)
*Level 2:* "Look, a dog is a dog. I'll get you a new one." (Not serious)
*Level 3:* "There is no way to help a kid get over a dead pet." (No solution)
*Level 4:* "I know you feel bad, but what can I do?" (No personal power)
*Empowering:* "I'm sorry the dog died and I'm sad. How are you feeling? If you want me to help you plan a funeral for him, I will." (Gives lots of comfort.)

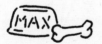

**A friend is hoping to get a promotion. I say:**

*Level 1:* "Look — some people don't even have a job." (No problem)
*Level 2:* "If you don't get it, you'll live." (Not serious)
*Level 3:* "Who knows how they decide on those promotions?" (No solution)
*Level 4:* "There is no way I can help." (No personal power)
*Empowering:* "I hope you get the promotion. Anything I can do to help you go after it?"

## THE RESPONSES

To practice identifying the four levels of discounting and empowering responses, read the following three examples and think about each response as you write in (1. No problem) (2. Not serious) (3. No solution) (4. No personal power) (5. Empowering). The first one is done for you.

**Teenager is mourning not having a date for a Friday night party and family member says:**

1. "I don't want to hear about it."

   _____
2. "It's not the Junior Prom you know."_____
3. "Look, it's too late for anybody to do anything to help you."

   _____
4. "I don't know how to help you."

   _____
5. "I love you. I'm sorry you don't have a date. Would you like to ask somebody over here Friday night?"_____

**Teenager wants a date, doesn't have one and says to self:**

1. "I don't care."

   _____
2. "The party probably won't be any fun anyway."_____
3. "If you don't just happen to get a date, there is nothing anyone can do."_____
4. "I can never get a date."

   _____
5. "I want to go to the party. I'll try three more ways to get a date. If I don't get one, I'll get somebody to go to a movie or watch TV with me."_____

**"I have heard that my friend's husband is sleeping with a variety of women. I am afraid my friend will get AIDS." I say:**

1. "Other people get AIDS, not *my* friends."_____
2. "The person who told me has been known to exaggerate. It's no big deal if he is seen with other women."_____
3. "However this couple is living their lives is up to them. It is no one else's business."

   _____
4. "I don't want to risk my friendship with her. Anyway, I wouldn't know what to say."

   _____
5. "This is serious, possibly life threatening information. I will find a way to check on it. Then, if I believe there is a good possibility it is true, I will find a time when she seems most likely to be able to hear this. I will tell her as gently as possible. I hate to risk our friendship, but I would never forgive myself if she got AIDS because she didn't know when I did."_____

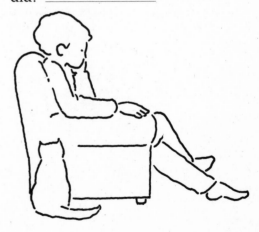

## Identify the Levels of Discounting

To practice identifying empowering responses and the different levels of discounting, choose one or more of the examples on the following chart and compare your answers to the ones suggested.

Remember that the level of discounting can change with the way words are delivered, the tone of voice, facial expression, and body language. Discounting may also be perceived as present or more severe discounting by people who have a history in their families or relationships of broken contracts and promises not kept. Treat these responses as suggestions and feel free to rewrite them if you wish.

Indicate the levels for each example by placing a 1, 2, 3, 4, or E in front of each response.

1. —Discounts existence of problem.
2. —Discounts seriousness of problem.
3. —Discounts solvability of problem.
4. —Discounts personal ability to solve problem.
E. —Empowering — takes other people, the situation, and the power of self into account.

---

**1. A two-year-old child runs into a busy street. The parent:**

\_\_\_\_ Says to self, *I've told him and told him and he doesn't pay attention, so what can I do?*

\_\_\_\_ Does not keep track of the child, does not notice.

\_\_\_\_ Runs and brings the child back and says seriously, "You must stay on the grass! Only cross the street with a big person." Watches child.

\_\_\_\_ "Nobody can keep kids that age from running in the street."

\_\_\_\_ Thinks, *Well, the cars usually go slowly on this street. They'll see him.*

*Suggested Answers: 4, 1, E, 3, 2*

**2. Teenager is driving twenty miles above speed limit. Three of her friends and her parent are in the car. The parent:**

\_\_\_\_ Thinks, *There is never a traffic cop when you need one.*

\_\_\_\_ Thinks, *She is driving. I have no right to embarrass her in front of her friends.*

\_\_\_\_ Doesn't notice.

\_\_\_\_ Says firmly, "Return to the speed limit and stay there or I will take the wheel." If teen does not slow down, parent makes her stop and parent drives. After they are home, parent sets rules and consequences for future driving.

\_\_\_\_ Parent thinks, "Well, all kids speed, I suppose."

*Suggested Answers: 3, 4, 1, E, 2*

**3. My beloved says, ''I want you to spend more time having fun with me.'' I say:**

____ "We spend lots of time together and we have enough fun."

____ "All right. Let's figure out how to do that."

____ "Most couples have difficulty finding enough time to play."

____ "Okay. . . I'll tell you a joke once a week."

____ "I'm really swamped for the rest of the month."

*Suggested Answers:* 1, E, 3, 2, 4

**4. My spouse has been hospitalized for a long time and I'm on the road a lot. I wonder how this is affecting our children. I say:**

____ "I make sure the kids and I are together when I'm home. I'm looking for a job where I can stay home. I have the best live-in care I can find. I've asked my sister to spend more time with my kids. I'm watching their behavior carefully and encouraging them to talk about their feelings."

____ "It can't be helped."

____ "Seven and nine year olds are old enough to take care of themselves."

____ "The kids haven't complained."

____ "Hey, I didn't plan it this way."

*Suggested Answers:* E, 3, 2, 1, 4

**5. A child is crying. Adult responds:**

____ "What is the matter? Can I help you?"

____ "I don't hear her."

____ "I like kids when they are smiling — I never know what to do with them when they cry."

____ "All kids cry."

____ "Look, if a kid feels like crying, there is nothing you can do."

*Suggested Answers:* E, 1, 4, 2, 3

**6. My son is single-minded in his devotion to the principles of his church. There is no room for discussion and he believes his church knows everything there is to know about right and wrong. He's very critical of other family members. Parent says:**

____ "I can't compete with the church."

____ "He's a very religious person and that's all that counts."

____ "I will listen respectfully to his beliefs and ask him to listen respectfully to mine. If he degrades my beliefs I will insist that he stop and I will change the subject."

____ "Once that church of his hooks people, that's the end of them."

____ "He has been through these phases before."

*Suggested Answers:* 4, 1, E, 3, 2

**7. You say people are supposed to ask for what they need. I respond:**

____ "If I have to ask for what I need, it doesn't count."

____ "Other people should know what I need."

____ "I know it's a myth to believe that others know what I need, so I will ask until I find someone who will help me get my needs met."

____ "I don't have any needs."

____ "I have some needs, but I'm surviving."

*Suggested Answers:* 4, 3, E, 1, 2

**8. My wife has two citations for driving while under the influence of alcohol and she is having trouble at work. I say:**

____ "At least she's drinking at home now and not out every night."

____ "I'll just keep on covering for her."

____ "Women are harder to treat than men."

____ "Thank goodness she is okay around me."

____ "I will stop protecting her and find out where she and I and our family can get the help we need and I will do it now."

*Suggested Answers:* 2, 4, 3, 1, E

**9. My daughter seems to pay much more attention to what her boyfriend wants than to what she wants. She carefully watches how he feels and frequently reassures and comforts him. He seems to like it, but doesn't return in kind. I say:**

____ "I get along fine with him."

____ "I will tell her about my observation of and concern for her behavior. I will ask her to read a book about the caretaking behaviors of codependency or join a women's group to get another perspective. I care too much about her not to say anything. I wish my parents had taught me to expect as much care as I am willing to give in a relationship."

____ "If I say anything it would make her angry and she might not have anything to do with me."

____ "What right have I to say anything? I did that myself until two years ago."

____ "That's what women have to do."

*Suggested Answers:* 1, E, 3, 4, 2

**10. My teenager is using drugs. Parent says:**

____ "He smokes dope now and then, that's all."

____ "I'll remind him that drug use is illegal and dangerous for him and he needs to stop using. I know I am not in control of his decision to use, but I can get help for him and for me. I will make whatever changes I need to make in my life and the way I respond to him."

____ "I don't know what to do, but I wish he'd straighten out."

____ "No. He's not."

____ "It's those darn kids he hangs around with."

*Suggested Answers:* 2, E, 4, 1, 3

**11. My love asks, ''Do you love me?'' I respond:**

____ "Don't embarrass me."

____ "Yes," (hug, hug, kiss, kiss) "I'm glad I live with you and I look forward to loving you and growing with you for the rest of my life."

____ "I gave you a valentine, didn't I? That should be enough."

____ "Oh, by the way, did you pay the gas bill?"

____ "It's impossible to get other people to really believe that you love them."

*Suggested Answers:* 4, E, 2, 1, 3

**12. My spouse looks at our child in a sexually suggestive way. They spend lots of time together without me. I say:**

____ "I have an uncomfortable feeling, but I'll ignore it and not say anything."

____ "You can't control what other people do when they are alone."

____ "I am disloyal for having suspicions and I wouldn't dare say anything anyway."

____ "I will remember that the adult is always the one who is responsible. I'll talk with my spouse and I will get some professional advice now. I will call a child protection agency if I need to."

____ "Parents are supposed to spend time with their kids and look at them and touch them."

*Suggested Answers:* 1, 3, 4, E, 2

**13. A friend says, ''I've been waiting to tell you about my great new ideas.'' I say:**

____ "I usually don't understand your great ideas."

____ "I'm busy right now, but I want to hear your idea. Can you wait until this evening to tell me?"

____ "I'll listen if there is nothing else to do."

____ "There is never enough time just to talk, is there?"

____ "I want to go to a movie tonight. Come with me?"

*Suggested Answers:* 4, E, 2, 3, 1

Remember, our task is not to kick ourselves if we have been discounting, but to learn to recognize it and stop it now.

## Ways to Change Discounting to Empowering

As you read the examples of the discounting levels, you may have thought of an area in which you are discounting. Use this next exercise to help you stop discounting and help you meet your needs and your children's needs.

● Review your recent behavior and identify two or three possible discounts.
● Select one incident of discounting to practice on. Pick the smallest, least threatening one. Remember that people discount to protect old decisions that have served them well but now need updating. Be gentle and loving with yourself. Notice, but do not blame yourself. This is a way to find out about yourself, not to find fault with yourself.

Describe your incident, and ask yourself these questions about your level of discounting:

*Level 1:* Am I ignoring a problem when there really is one?
*Level 2:* Am I pretending this problem is not serious when it may well be, or am I making more of this than is necessary?
*Level 3:* Am I assuming there is no solution to this problem when there may be several and I haven't asked for help?
*Level 4:* Am I backing off from this because I don't want to face the implications of solving it?

● Identify the level at which you discounted.
● Brainstorm possible empowering actions you could have taken.
● Predict which one might be most successful and decide how you will handle a similar situation in the future. Are there amends you can make now?
● When you notice you are doing fourth level discounting — "I can't do anything" — remember that people usually can do something. Think of four things you can do, then pick one and do it.

If you notice that you are doing third level discounting — "There is no solution," or "There are no other options" — run, don't walk, for help. The yellow section of the phone book, a supportive friend, counselor, clergyperson, book, or class are places to get more information about possible solutions.

If you are consistently discounting on the first or second level, welcome that information. It's an indication that you once made a survival decision to ignore some information, possible actions, or some feelings. Honor yourself for having decided to block what was too overwhelming back then. Realize the blocking that helped you then, and often gets you in trouble now. Get whatever help, spiritual support, counseling, or support group help you need to reclaim your ability to hear and see situations accurately and to act upon them. (See "How to Find a Support Group or a Therapist," Appendix B.) Meanwhile:

- Practice empowering, paying attention, seeing and hearing and feeling what is really going on, not what you hope or wish is going on.
- Think about the points on the Structure Chart. Every time you use Rigidity, Marshmallowing, or Abandonment, you are discounting on some level. Every time you use appropriate Nonnegotiable Rules and Negotiable Rules, you are empowering.
- Think about the points on the Nurture Chart. Every time you use Abuse, Conditional Care, Indulgence, or Neglect, you are discounting on some level. Every time you use appropriate Assertive Care and Supportive Care, you are empowering.
- Affirm yourself.
- Grieve, with support, the losses that led you to start discounting.
- Look for new information or make a decision or form a new way of thinking of yourself that will support your right to be powerful and successful.
- Identify where you are taking self, others, and the situation into full account. Celebrate! Build on your strengths.

# CHAPTER 6

# *Stop Discounting*

There are many ways of belittling people. Who among us has not cringed from derisive laughter, cruel teasing, sarcasm, and ridicule? Abuse and abandonment are profound ways of discounting. Let us sharpen our sensitivity to each of the practices and replace them all with love. Let us look at the underlying decisions that support discounting, and find ways to get off the merry-go-round and on with healthy lives.

### Laughter

Laughter can either block healing or it can be healing. In *The Anatomy of an Illness,*[4] Norman Cousins describes how he used laughter to recover from a serious illness. Joyous laughter at a joke that disparages no one, or laughing in an empathetic way builds esteem and offers intimacy. It invites people to feel special and signals that they are "insiders." As an example: Charlie brought flowers to his wife for her birthday, not realizing he was one week early. Ginny and the children genuinely enjoyed the surprise of his "mistake" and he joined in the laughter.

But laughter can also discount, alienate, and disconnect when it puts people "on the outside." Look at the following situations and think how the laughter would sound at each of the four levels of discounting.

**You fall and break your tailbone. The pain is intense.**
*Discounting:*
*Level 1:* "Ha, ha, ha." (No problem)
*Level 2:* "Chuckle, chuckle. Some fancy spill you took there." (Not serious)

*Level 3:* "Ha, ha, people fall on those steps every time it drops below freezing." (No solution to this problem, there are no options)

*Level 4:* "I'm glad it wasn't me who fell. Ha, ha, ha." (No personal power)

Compare these with the empowering, responsible response: "Are you hurt? Can I help you?"

When someone is hurt, laughter is never appropriate — not even nervous laughter.

Laughing at pain is sometimes defended as "having a sense of humor." Any laughter that happens at the expense of someone's safety or self-esteem is destructive, not humorous. That includes laughing or smiling at our own distress. We may sometimes laugh ruefully at the human condition as we reflect on our past ineptness, but this kind of forgiving laughter comes only after anger, sadness, grieving, and acceptance of the situation and of one's humanity are completed.

## Parental Laughter

Being laughed at is one of the cruelest ways of being discounted because it ridicules the person at the same time it discounts the problem. It is a form of abuse. Hurtful parental laughter can ring in the ears of a child for days, and that same long-forgotten laughter, years later, triggers the old messages, *You are not important. Don't dare to get close.* This laughter engenders timidity, withdrawal, rebellion, and other habits of thought and behavior that are harmful to self and others. The message of such laughter is that familial love and support are scarce or unreliable. Before you laugh at a child's mishap that seems amusing to you, stop to think: *Will the child find this as funny as I do or is it painful to her?* Wait to see if the child laughs. If the mishap is truly not serious or painful you can laugh together.

## Children Who Laugh at Their Own Pain

Disparaging laughter is especially harmful to children. When they are laughed at disrespectfully, they learn to laugh at their pain in an attempt to be one of the "in group" or "in" the family.

If a child smiles or laughs at his own pain, either physical or emotional, before he acts hurt or confused or embarrassed, stop and take stock. Has he already learned that he is supposed to laugh at his pain? If so, you can expect him to neglect to take care of himself because he has learned to discount the information that pain sends: that he is to do something to protect or care for or heal himself.

What can a parent do to discourage children from laughing or smiling at themselves in discounting, self-destructive ways?

- Stop laughing at pain or mishaps, or at dangerous, mean, or destructive behavior yourself.
- Say, in a loving way, "That does not seem funny to me," or "Let's talk about what we can do to help you instead of laughing at your problem, pain, embarrassment, or mistake," or "I feel uncomfortable when you laugh at pain," or "Please don't do that."

If your young child is in a play group that expects him to laugh at his own pain, do something. Tell the other kids to stop. Enlist the aid of other adults. Find a new play group for the child. Change day-care or nursery schools. Move if that is the only way you can stop the laughing at pain.

If a junior high school child is engaging in the frequent ridicule practiced by her group, teach her that this is common behavior among kids her age, that it is destructive, that you expect her to outgrow it shortly, and not to use it at home.

If, in spite of your parental love and Structure, your child continues to smile about her own misfortune or misbehavior, that is a signal that the child has internalized being discounted and is now internally discounting herself. Get whatever help you need, including therapy, to get this discounting stopped before you are faced with even more serious behaviors.

*Gallows Smile*

Eric Berne, the father of Transactional Analysis,[5] called an unconscious smile at our own pain a "gallows smile" because we are, in effect, smiling at our own destruction. The name comes from the practice of having a condemned person on the gallows, telling a joke as the rope is placed around his neck so the crowd will be laughing as he dies.

As awful as it sounds, many of us do smile at our pain and misfortune. Such smiles are a signal that we have touched some early area of our lives where our needs were not met, nor could we get them met, so we learned to discount them. Our smiles signal that we are still discounting those needs and ourselves. It was a situation we had to accept then. It is understandable that we decided whatever we did in order to stay alive and grow. But, if years later, we are still smiling about pain and about not getting what we need, and it keeps us from being responsible to ourselves and others, it is a poor decision to hold on to. We need to stop smiling at pain and take action to alleviate it.

To find out if you are using gallows smiles and laughter and modeling them for your child, ask a friend to report to you if she notices you smiling or laughing at something painful or disturbing. Choose a friend who will report honestly, with love, and who will not use this opportunity to "get" you. If you aren't sure about a friend, ask a counselor or therapist to help you with this.

Talk about what concerns you most about your life or your family, and your friend or counselor can soon tell you if you are smiling inappropriately. If you are, welcome this as a physical signal that you are doing internal discounting. At first you may want to deny the smile, or you may feel angry or embarrassed about it. Remember that a gallows smile or laugh is usually done outside of your awareness. Now that you are aware of it, you can change it!

*Gallows Smile? Not Me!*

If you have ever wanted to deny a gallows smile when you were told about one, check your discounting response with these examples of the four discounting levels.

**Your friend or counselor says: "You asked me to tell you if you smiled when you described pain, embarrassment, or failure. Did you know that you smiled when you told me you failed your test?"**

*Level 1:* "I didn't smile." (There is no problem)
*Level 2:* "How can you turn a little smile into such a big deal?" (Not serious)
*Level 3:* "Everybody laughs at that sort of thing — nobody wants to see a grown person cry." (No solution)
*Level 4:* "I can't help it. Sometimes my mouth just smiles." (No personal power)

Watching your own gallows smile on videotape is a compelling way to face the truth. If you have no video, check your physical response by placing your fingers firmly on either side of your mouth to feel your smile. Repeat what you said when you smiled. If you feel your cheek muscles push for the smile, press firmly with your fingers to prevent the smile and repeat what you said before. Notice as soon as you prevent your smile, you stop discounting your sadness, fear, anger, or whatever you were denying. Now you are ready to get on with the healing of that particular pain.

Remember, as you learn to stop using discounting types of laughter, you create lots of opportunities in your life for delightful, healing, joyous laughter.

### Teasing

Teasing, like laughter, can build esteem and encourage intimacy or it can cruelly discount. To tease is to irritate, provoke, annoy, disturb, deceive, or ridicule, according to most definitions. Used this way, teasing is sometimes an attempt to make ourselves look better at someone else's expense. Any time we are tempted to tease, in a hurtful way, it is important to stop and do something healthy instead. Teasing, offered to children instead of needed information, rules, or love, is damaging.

A kind of harmless teasing between people who feel secure with themselves and each other is often called banter, pleasantry, or joking. The message it sends is, *I like you, I want to laugh with you (not at you); here's a funny way of telling you that I care about you or that I notice you.* This kind of banter is friendly, even loving. Nevertheless, be very cautious about its use. People who grew up with hurtful teasing often misunderstand and are offended by it, even if they pretend to be jolly about it. Also, since children under six are working at the developmental task of separating reality from fantasy they may miss the friendly intent of this kind of teasing unless there are some very broad hints such as winks, big smiles, or little rituals that assure that this is joking and not ridicule.

Benjamin's daddy knows how to do this. Four-year-old Benjamin came racing into the house, interrupted his father who was watching TV, placed himself squarely in front of his dad and announced, "I had an ice cream cone."

His dad asked quizzically, "You did?"

Benjy replied seriously, "Yes,"

His dad said, "Did you bring me one?"

Benjy shouted, "No!"

The father jumped to his feet and shouted, in a singsong voice, "How could you do that? You turkey! You know I love ice cream cones! What shall I do to you because you didn't bring me ice cream?"

Benjy shouted delightedly, "Restle me!"

Dad and son rolled on the floor, wrestling, hugging, and laughing.

Here are aspects that made the teasing positive:

- The child initiated it.
- Dad was willing to be interrupted.
- Dad paid attention to Benjamin's invitation to play.
- Dad exaggerated his actions by jumping up and shouting in a special, ritualized way.
- Dad and Benjy ended the interlude with positive touch and laughter.

### Sarcasm and Ridicule

Sarcasm and ridicule are forms of discounting that strike at the being of a person. They issue a bitter and mocking invitation for contemptuous laughter which says, "You are not important and your needs are not serious." Because sarcasm and ridicule are difficult to counter and leave people feeling ashamed, exposed, stupid, or diminished, these forms of discounting should not be excused as friendly teasing.

Sarcasm and ridicule command an instant response from children and thus may seem momentarily attractive to parents. But parents may not realize that criticism, sarcasm, and ridicule not only stop unwanted behaviors, they also wither important aspects of a child's growth. Think about Karla's response: She was in the backseat of the car, chatting merrily with her mother about the school day. Grandpa, riding in front, said scornfully, "She's some talker, isn't she?" Karla didn't speak for the rest of the drive and would not respond to her mother's request to finish the story. It is healthier for everyone when adults replace ridicule and sarcasm with instruction. Tell children what you want them to do and how to do it. And remember, such instruction works better with adults too.

### Using Sarcasm to Toughen?

Some people believe sarcasm toughens children. The theory is that, if children can learn to survive sarcasm at home and in the play group, they will be able to let it roll off when they get it in the outside world. On the surface, this seems to work. But, people trained this way pay a price. They often use ridicule in their relationships and against themselves.

Girls who are ridiculed for not being as good at math as boys often believe it and do not extend themselves to become proficient in math. These girls may even mistrust other women who are good at math. When boys are ridiculed for being sensitive, they learn to hide their sensitivity or sometimes lose it. Members of minority groups sometimes trash themselves — they do to themselves and each other what their oppressors have done to them. Players of "Dozens," a game used by street kids to prove their toughness, hurl scathing insults at each other until one player breaks down and loses face. You can read more about it in *The Jesus Bag*[6] by William Grier and Price Cobbs.

Think about people who learn to use put-downs skillfully; they continue to put down themselves and their peers.

Wouldn't it be better to change the culture so people don't learn to expect and honor ridicule, sarcasm, and other discounts?

### Double Binds — Messages that Create Dilemmas

Double binds are especially confusing and immobilizing discounts. They discount by saying two things that, when considered individually, are understandable, but when offered as a pair, are impossible to reconcile. They are mutually exclusive experiences and both true.

Double binds discount the other person by creating a box, a corner, or a Catch-22, where that person can do no right. They discount the self by creating life situations that yield confusion and pain rather than support and joy. In *Adult Children of Alcoholics*, Janet Woititz[7] lists double-bind messages that are common in families where alcohol is abused.

- "I love you." / "Go away."
- "You can't do anything right." / "I need you."
- "Always tell the truth." / "I don't want to know."
- "I'll be there for you." / "I promise I'll be there next time."
- "Everything is fine, don't worry." / "How can I deal with all of this."
- "Being drunk isn't okay." / "Anything a drunk does is okay."

If these messages sound normal, or if you want to learn more about understanding and countering them, use the exercises at the end of the book (See "Getting Free of Double Binds," Appendix A) to help you recognize, counter, and avoid double binds.

A common double bind offered by parents is "I will take care of you." / and then, I don't take care of you. It is easy for parents to say "I will take care of you" and mean it. But if those same parents didn't have helpful, loving parenting themselves, they won't know how to give care well. If they do not face up to that reality and learn how, the double bind becomes the padlock on the family album, keeping the secret of neglect or abuse and passing it along.

## Abandonment

Abandonment of any kind is a first level discount of the other person. It is probably the most serious way that parents can discount children. Abandonment implies, *Caring for you is not important — you do not exist,* or, *I wish you didn't exist.* The child interprets the behavior of a parent who leaves, is drunk, or is preoccupied, as abandonment.

Sometimes a parent abandons a child by refusing to accept her as she is. "We wanted a boy, but Ashley does very well. She is quite a tomboy." In this sad circumstance the child often attempts to make sense of a no-sense situation by taking the blame on herself for not being a boy. This is called *victim blame* because the child is the victim but she blames herself. This kind of self-blame as a child perpetuates itself in adult life. As an adult, Ashley needs to stop blaming herself, stop pretending what her parents did was okay, deliberately sort out what really happened, and find the support and healing she needs and deserves.

## Underlying Decisions that Lead to Denial and Discounting

Denial and discounting protect previously made decisions. You can practice understanding how discounting and empowering spring from old decisions or beliefs by looking at the following examples and guessing what the underlying decision for each might be. There is also an empowering response for which you can guess an underlying decision or attitude.

**Pat's friend has asked: "Will you help me with the decorations for my club party?" Pat responds:**

*Level 1:* "You are always doing something for that club. You should spend as much time with me." (No problem)

*Level 2:* "They don't need decorations to have a party." (Not serious)
*Level 3:* "Decorating is a lot of work. There isn't time to get it done." (No solution)
*Level 4:* "I'm no good at artsy-craftsy things." (No personal power)
*Empowering:* "Sure. What do you want me to do?" Or "No, I can't commit to do that, but I hope you find someone to help you."

Guess what the underlying decision for each response might be.

1.
2.
3.
4.
E.

Compare your guesses with this possible list.

1.  My needs are more desperate than yours.
2.  I need to do things perfectly and I feel ashamed if I don't.
3.  I am not artistic.
4.  I can't decorate well enough and someone would criticize me.
E.  I am competent.

Other decisions that could account for all four of the above levels of discounting might be:

● I am an artistic klutz.
● I don't dare to get close. If I help people once, they bug me forever.
● It is not okay for me to say no directly.
● This person might get to know me better if we do this together and I can't risk being known.
● I am not important so I am jealous of people who belong to clubs.
● This person might want to be intimate and I don't know how to be intimate as a friend. I only know about sexual intimacy.

Remember when other people discount you, it makes no difference what their reason is, it is your responsibility to deal with the discount without discounting them in return.

We can continue to identify our underlying decisions and beliefs. Some of the ways we can do that are by exploring the dynamics of our families of origin, by noticing what bothers us so much in others, by journaling, by attending to our feelings and letting them guide us to thoughts and memories, and by therapy.

**New Decisions**

If you uncover those old decisions and the situations that led to them and expose them to the light of day, you will discover yourself as a child whose needs were not met, a child who made lifesaving decisions anyway. Applaud those decisions. Grieve the situation and make new decisions that will help you take better care of yourself and others now.

Robert Subby in *Lost in the Shuffle*[8] calls children who had to make unfortunate decisions "victims," but adults who continue to base their current actions upon them "volunteers." Perhaps you are tired of being a volunteer discounter, but find it hard to maintain new, empowering behaviors because the old decisions keep playing in your head, tugging you back to old behaviors. Here are some of the ways people have helped themselves find new attitudes and behaviors and make new decisions:

- Laura read and used self-help books.
- Ron took parenting classes.
- Stephanie told her story in her support groups and got suggestions for making new decisions.
- Marty did therapy.
- Fred participated in grief workshops.
- Alice used her Twelve Step support group.
- Connie did all of the above and more.

We all have different life-affirming tasks to accomplish and will choose different ways to do them. This book, the class, the program, the therapist are there to help. It is up to us to take the risk and the discomfort, to do the grieving and make the changes. Since it is damaging to stay stuck and not change, let yourself be worth the discomfort, the determination, the discipline, and the effort to grow. The rewards are inner peace, health, happiness, and joy. Another great reward for changing is the satisfaction that we are improving the parenting legacy we pass on to our kids.

Remember, we do change. We can't stay the same — we are either growing and expanding, or we are tightening our defensive denials every day.

## Getting Off the Merry-Go-Round

Here are some questions people often ask about discounting. You may have been wondering about them yourself.

*What if I realize that other people are discounting me?*

Stop to think if you are discounting yourself or your needs in some way. Then decide what you want to change in this situation. Usually, if we are clear about our needs, desires, skills, and goals we can think of several options for managing the discounts of others without discounting ourselves or them.

*My world is filled with discounts. How can I remember to recognize them?*

As you use the thinking techniques in this chapter to identify discounts, be aware of your feelings. You may have a clutch in your stomach or tightening of your throat when you receive a discount. Or you may have a sneaky feeling of relief when you seem to get by with a discount. Acknowledge and learn from these feelings or any other sensation you have. You can learn to trust your feelings to help you know when you are discounting or being discounted. You can use them to remind you to take responsibility for yourself.

*So many people discount. Isn't it normal and can't we just ignore it?*

No and no. With people, "frequent" doesn't necessarily mean normal. It is normal for members of families to help each other survive, to treat each other with love, support, and respect. If we have lost that birthright, we need to reclaim our right to be treated and treat people this way and stop our discounting. True, there are many discounts in the world around us. In some situations there are too many for us to deal with and we may have to change jobs or friends.

*What can I do to help my family?*

Improve your ability to nurture and structure others and yourself. Teach family members to give warm nurture and clear structure to you. Replace your discounting behavior with responsible parenting.

*There is a big problem in our family and we don't talk about it. Is this discounting?*

Yes. You may not feel like facing up to it either. You may feel too scared or mortified to even mention it, so your family treats it as a secret. Often, big family problems stem from some unfinished business. That is the time to get some outside help.

Sometimes two or more people have made outside-of-our-awareness secret contracts, such as, "I won't mention what you are doing if you don't notice what I am doing," or "I'll ignore your drinking problem if you don't confront my martyrdom," or "I won't mention your cocaine use if you don't notice my sexual addiction," or "I'll ignore your overeating if you accommodate my workaholism," or "I won't mention your frequent absences if you don't get mad at my gambling." These are examples of mutual discounting agreements.

The first person in this kind of double-destruct contract to become aware of it should run, not walk, for competent outside help and do everything possible to resolve the problem. Even with goodwill and determination to get well, the people in this kind of relationship usually need strong outside support over time to help develop more satisfying and loving relationships. (See "How to Find a Support Group or a Therapist," Appendix B.)

*How can I stop discounting and start empowering?*

Read through the following list of actions. Select two or three to start doing, and do them. When you are ready, add others.

- Start by accepting yourself as human. All people discount sometimes.
- Honor yourself for having decided to block, deny, or accept victim blame when that was the only choice you could make to survive.
- Accept the fact that old, once helpful blocks often get us in trouble now.
- Set some long-term goals to empower, to stop discounting, in several areas important to you and your family. Set a short-time goal to change one of those areas.
- Use empowering responses or initiate responsible action at least once every day for a week. Do not be deterred if you feel awkward. Remember, if you do not stumble as you learn this new skill, you will probably be the first person in the history of the world to achieve instant competence without practice.

- Encourage yourself and your children to be responsible by using responsible language that avoids discounting and indicates clearly who is to do what. (See "Encouraging Responsibility through Language," Appendix A.)
- Get outside support. Join a therapy group, a support group, a Twelve Step group. Get a friend, who won't discount the area you are working on, to cheer for you and plan celebrations for you.
- During the next week, add a new area.
- Plan celebrations to mark your successes.
- Use a journal to record your progress.
- Think about how discounting creates scarcities in your life. Decide to go for abundance.
- Use a Fuss Box (see Appendix A) or other method of accepting, expressing, and letting go of anger and use that energy on problem-solving.
- If you have big trouble replacing a particular discount with empowering, get some therapeutic help in identifying and remaking the underlying decision.
- Ask a friend to point out discounts to you only if you trust that person will do so with love and will never, never use that contract as an opportunity to get you, get even, embarrass you, or hurt you.
- Likewise, do not use your knowledge of discounting to blame or shame others. Find solutions to problems without using accusations, name-calling, or put-downs.
- Be in charge of updating your beliefs to form the life base most helpful for you and your family now.
- Love yourself, discounting and all.

*Will doing less discounting help my parenting?*

Greatly. The less you discount, the better you parent. The unspoken contract between parents and children is that parents will nurture and structure, and children will learn and grow.

It is important for us to remember that although it is easier to overcome third level (no solution) and fourth level (personal power) discounts, *from the child's point of view all levels amount to total discounting.* The child's problem remains unsolved; the child's need remains unmet.

**If the child has a punctured foot it matters not if the parent says:**
*Level 1:* "It doesn't look injured to me." (No problem)
*Level 2:* "It doesn't look serious. Just forget it."
(Not serious)
*Level 3:* "There is no help for an injury like that so ignore it."
(No solution)
*Level 4:* "Oh, dear, that looks awful, but I don't know what to do for a puncture wound." (No personal power)

The foot is still injured. The child is still unattended, uncomforted, and neglected.

When we, as parents, discount needed care for our children on any level, we break our part of the parenting contract.

When we attend, when we look, listen, ask, think, and act to provide Structure and Nurture for our children, we keep our part of the parenting contract, even when we don't do it perfectly. The contract is not about being perfect. It is about doing the best we can on the day we are living right now.

# Growing Up Again and Again and Again

*Not many years ago I began to play the cello. Most people would say that what I am doing is "learning to play" the cello. But these words carry into our minds the strange idea that there exists two very different processes: 1) learning to play the cello; and 2) playing the cello. They imply that I will do the first until I have completed it, at which point I will stop the first process and begin the second; in short, that I will go on "learning to play" until I have "learned to play" and that then I will begin to play. Of course, this is nonsense. There are not two processes, but one. We learn to do something by doing it. There is no other way.*

**— John Holt, author of *How Children Fail*,
and others wrote this in a newsletter**

# CHAPTER 7

# Ages and Stages

"It's just a stage she is going through. It's not important. Just ignore her and she'll forget it soon." That is what Mother said when Lois was eight and stubbornly pursued some interest that inconvenienced another family member. Was mother right? Partly. Mother was right about stages, but wrong about their importance. We all go through stages as we grow and *each stage is important*. Children and adults need to be supported, not ignored, in their mastery of the developmental growth tasks for each stage.

Lois forgot what happened, but the skills she learns and the decisions she made at each stage remain with her unless overshadowed by later, bigger events or unless, as an adult, Lois deliberately decides to change them.

## What Is a Stage?

A developmental stage is a describable segment of growing up. During each segment of time, the person is busy with age-appropriate tasks that help answer the all-important questions: Who am I? And who am I in relation to others? How do I acquire the skills that I need?

We will use seven stages to describe development, but since each person has her own timetable for growth, the ages listed are approximations. The main goals for the stages are the resolution of the following questions:

*Stage One (Being) — birth to about 6 months*

Is it okay for me to be here, to make my needs known and to be cared for?

*Stage Two (Doing) — about 6 to about 18 months*
Is it safe for me to explore and try new things and to trust what I learn?
*Stage Three (Thinking) — about 18 months to about 3 years*
Is it okay for me to learn to think for myself?
*Stage Four (Identity and Power) — about 3 years to about 6 years*
Is it okay for me to be who I am, with my unique abilities? Is it okay for me to find out who others are, and learn the consequences of my behavior?
*Stage Five (Structure) — about 6 years to about 12 years*
How do I build an internal Structure that supports me and others? How do I develop the competence to master the technical and social skills I need to live in my culture?
*Stage Six (Identity, Sexuality, and Separation) — about 13 years to about 19 years*
How can I become a separate person with my own values and still belong? Is it okay for me to be independent, to honor my sexuality, and to be responsible?
*Stage Seven (Interdependence) — adult*
How will I balance my needs for competence, for intimacy and separateness, and how will I move from independence to interdependence?

The experiences and decisions made at each developmental stage shapes an adult's ability to offer and receive Nurture and Structure.

## The Nurture-Structure Shield

How would you describe your ability to care for yourself and others if you were to think of it as having a concrete shape? Would it be an umbrella? A cloak? A bubble of white light? A shield?

We will use a shield as a symbol for the skills we use to nurture and structure ourselves and others. If you think of your ability as something else, as a cloak for example, each time you read "shield" change it to "cloak" so it will fit for you.

Our shields are built from the accumulation of our experiences in each developmental stage. By examining our experiences and decisions from each stage, we can see the many skills we have developed that are working well for us, and we can also see the holes, the gaps we need to repair or fill in. If you would like to try a visualization exercise to picture your shield, cloak, or whatever you choose to call it, use the guided imagery exercise at the end of the book. (See "See-

110

ing Our Own Shields — A Visualization," Appendix B.)

When children experience consistent, loving, even parenting, they have the opportunity to build strong shields. But such consistent loving only comes from mature, dedicated, healthy parents whose parenting efforts are continuous. Many of us grew up with adults whose energy was diverted from us by alcohol, other drugs, or other addictions such as food, relationships, work, or religion. For these and many other reasons (for example, war, poverty, illness), our parents weren't able to meet our needs adequately. They may have neglected or abused us physically, sexually, or psychologically because of their own pain or inhibited development.

It is interesting that although such families suffer from very different problems, the effects of uneven parenting are much the same.

From the outside, for example, a family with a member addicted to alcohol may look very different than a family that is addicted to rigid religious practices or one struggling to care for a chronic invalid. In the end, the dynamics of neglect are often the same: children in those situations lack the opportunity to develop the Nurture and Structure that builds strong shields.

Also, our shields, like a tree, are strongest if they have a healthy center. The center is the part we acquired during childhood. If there are holes in the center part, we have probably learned to deny and discount our needs or defend our early decisions. Such decisions, which were necessary at one time, can be damaging to us now. We need to begin repairing those holes or weak spots now.

### What Is Growing Up Again?

Growing up again and again is getting what we missed earlier so we don't have to go on living without what we need now. We grow up again so we can do better parenting, so we can feel more alive. Growing up again is the process of choosing *one* small hole at a time in our shield and filling it in, or repairing one small corner of a large hole.

"But, I don't want to grow up again," you might say. "Isn't it enough that I got through it the first time? Who wants to go back and relive old pain?" Claudia Black points out in her book *It Will Never Happen To Me*[1] that we must go back or it does happen again. The pain, the old behavior, the old patterns, never really get resolved unless we go back, unless we grow up again.

Fortunately, growing up again is about going forward. It is the process of being active in ways that help us make new decisions and use new behaviors.

For some of us, the holes or gaps in our shield are large enough and deep enough that the kinds of activities suggested here are not enough to repair them. We must add the kind of repair work done in therapy.

## How Do We Know When We Need to Grow Up Again?

There are several signals that let adults know it is time to do some growing up again. You may suspect you have a hole in your shield if an uncomfortable number of the discounting examples sounded all too familiar, or if Structure still sounds like criticism, or if you continue to reject Nurture.

There are several ways to grow up again. Sometimes we teach ourselves how to grow up again as we learn to parent our children well. Living with children who are working on specific developmental tasks seems to stimulate parents to rework those same tasks. For example, when a two-year-old is saying no and being resistant, the parents often find themselves feeling resistant and refurbishing their ability to say no and to think independently.

We also strengthen our shields as we experience the rhythms of our own growth, moving through the developmental tasks of our adult years at the same time we recycle earlier tasks in more sophisticated ways. Pamela Levins' helpful theory of recycling is described in her book, *Becoming the Way We Are.*[2] You can use this section of the book to help you assess, by developmental stage, the strengths and holes in your shield.

When we missed a lot the first time we grew up, when the holes in our shields are large, we often need the help of competent support groups, therapists, or therapy groups to help us with our healing. (See "How to Find a Support Group Or a Therapist," Appendix B.)

## Stay Underwhelmed

Many of us, when we get a glimpse of what we can do to improve our lives, want to do it all at once. We want to be finished last week. Some of us may even have gone to a therapist and said, "Fix me. NOW."

We want to grow up fast.

It doesn't work like that. It works more like this: a sharp

upward growth swing, and then a plateau while we consolidate new skills, attitudes, and beliefs. Often there is a little back-slipping or turmoil before we start the next growth swing. If you feel discouraged, remember that as you grow up again, each plateau is higher than the last. Growing up again is a process, not a onetime accomplishment. When you feel impatient, repeat to yourself:

- One hole at a time.
- One task at a time.
- One experience at a time.
- One new decision at a time.
- One new behavior at a time.
- One day at a time.

Each hole that you repair will strengthen your entire shield and make future growing up again work easier. Behold yourself with your eyes filled with wonder and appreciation. Remember that you can be scared and still think and go ahead. Healing involves grieving for what you had or did not have. Part of the grief work will include facing your anger and frustration. Eventually you will reach the place where you can notice another bit of repair work and say, "Okay. What is it I am to learn now? I may as well get on with it."

Meanwhile, you can grow at your own pace. Stay underwhelmed.

## Using the Charts

You can use the charts on the next pages to remind you of what your children need and what you need. Each chart includes a brief list of important *developmental tasks* for that particular stage, *behaviors common to children* that age, *affirmations* focusing on the tasks of that stage, *parent behaviors that are helpful*, and ones that are *unhelpful* for children that age. *Clues to growing up again* includes a sample of attitudes and behaviors that can indicate the need for adults to rework developmental tasks from that stage. *Activities that support growing up again* are examples of small and big things that adults can do to support healing and growing. *Affirmations for self* are messages that promote healing and growth.

If you are familiar with the power of affirmations, you will already know that you can use the developmental affirmations as a springboard to help you identify the exact messages that you and your children need. The complete list is at the end of the book. (See "Developmental Affirmations: How to Use Them with Your Family and Yourself," Appendix B.)

If you are being introduced to affirmations for the first time, a few words about them are in order. An affirmation is anything we say or do for others to let them know that we believe they are lovable and capable. Affirming encourages self-esteem. But the affirmations we deliver to others must be sincere or they become crazy-making double-bind messages.

Self-affirmations are all the things we say, do, think, and feel, externally and internally, that indicate we are lovable and capable. Self-affirming builds our self-esteem and self-love and can be especially important when we are tempted to discount our needs and not believe that the affirmations are important or true for us. We can start using the developmental affirmations by saying the messages to ourselves as "you" messages, speaking from our own nurturing parent to the child within us — "I'm glad you're alive."

Later, we can affirm ourselves with an "I" message, when the child within is willing to make that statement as a celebration or to claim that statement as a conviction that the inner child does believe or wants to believe — "I'm glad I'm alive."

It is important to use "I" messages to ourselves only when *we* have chosen them and not because someone else told us to say them that way. Self-esteem cannot be built around the desire to please someone else; it is an internal process about an internal set of beliefs. Affirming ourselves and visualizing ourselves as if the affirmations we have chosen are already true helps us make them so.

. (There are specific affirming messages we need to hear and learn to give at each stage of growth. See "Developmental Affirmations: How to Use Them," Appendix B.)

Affirmations can be delivered by look, word, or deed. They can be offered as gifts, said, sung, or acted upon. There is more information about affirmations in the book, *Self-Esteem: A Family Affair*[3] by Jean Illsley Clarke.

## Stage One — Being from Birth to about 6 Months

The first stage is about deciding to be, to live, to thrive, to trust, to call out to have needs met, to expect to have needs met, to be joyful. These decisions are important to nourish and amplify throughout our whole lives.

*1. Job of the child (developmental tasks)*

- To call for care.
- To cry or otherwise signal to get needs met.
- To accept touch.
- To accept Nurture.
- To bond emotionally, to learn to trust caring adults and self.
- To decide to live, to be.

*2. Typical behaviors of the child*

- Cries or fusses to make needs known.
- Cuddles.
- Makes lots of sounds.
- Looks at and responds to faces, especially eyes.
- Imitates.

*3. Affirmations for being*

- I'm glad you are alive.
- You belong here.
- What you need is important to me.
- I'm glad you are you.
- You can grow at your own pace.
- You can feel all of your feelings.
- I love you and I care for you willingly.

*4. Helpful parent behaviors*

- Affirm the child for doing developmental tasks.
- Provide loving, consistent care.
- Respond to infant's needs.
- Think for the baby.
- Hold and look at baby while feeding.
- Nurture by touching, looking, talking, and singing.
- Get help when unsure of how to care for baby.
- Be reliable and trustworthy.
- Get others to nurture you.
- For additional helpful parent behaviors, see *Help! for Parents of Infants.*[4]

*5. Unhelpful parent behaviors*

- Not responding to the baby's signals.
- Not touching or holding enough.
- Rigid, angry, agitated responses.
- Feeding before baby signals.
- Punishment.
- Lack of healthy physical environment.
- Lack of protection, including from older siblings.
- Criticizing child for anything.
- Discounting.

116

*6. Clues to a need for adults to grow up again*

- Not trusting others.
- Wanting others to know what you need without your asking.
- Not knowing what you need.
- Not needing anything. Feeling numb.
- Believing others needs are more important than yours.
- Not trusting others to come through for you.
- Not wanting to be touched, or either compulsive touching or joyless sexual touching.
- Unwillingness to disclose information about self, especially negative information.

*7. Activities that support growing up again*

- Use and adapt this stage's "Helpful parent behaviors" to care for your inner child.
- Take a warm bath and get a therapeutic massage.
- Sing lullabies to the little child in you.
- Get more hugs.
- Close your eyes. Visualize yourself as a child. If the all-perfect mother or father could see this child right now, what would she or he do? What would she or he say? Do those things and say those things to yourself or ask someone who loves you to do or say those things for you.
- Do something to make your house more comfortable.
- Get therapy if you need it.

*8. Growing up again affirmations for being (when you feel ready)*

- I'm glad I am alive.
- I belong here.
- What I need is important.
- I'm glad I am me.
- I grow at my own pace.
- I feel all of my feelings.
- I love and care for myself and willingly accept love and care from others.

117

## Stage Two — Doing
## From about 6 to about 18 Months

Stage Two — the "doing" stage — is a powerful time when it is important for the child to decide to trust others, that it is safe and wonderful to explore, to trust his senses, to know what he knows, to be creative and active, and to get support while doing all these things.

### 1. *Job of the child (developmental tasks)*

- To explore and experience the environment.
- To develop sensory awareness by using all senses.
- To signal needs; to trust others and self.
- To continue forming secure attachments with parents.
- To get help in times of stress.
- To start to learn that there are options and not all problems are easily solved.
- To develop initiative.
- To continue tasks from Stage One.

### 2. *Typical behaviors of the child*

- Tests all senses by exploring the environment.
- Is curious.
- Is easily distracted.
- Wants to explore on own but be able to retrieve caregiver at will.
- Starts patty-cake and peek-a-boo.
- Starts using words during middle or latter part of stage.

### 3. *Affirmations for doing*

- You can explore and experiment and I will support and protect you.
- You can use all of your senses when you explore.
- You can do things as many times as you need to.
- You can know what you know.
- You can be interested in everything.
- I like to watch you initiate and grow and learn.
- I love you when you are active and when you are quiet.

### 4. *Helpful parent behaviors*

- Affirm child for doing developmental tasks.
- Continue to offer love, safety, and protection.
- Provide a safe environment.
- Protect child from harm.
- Continue to provide food, nurturing touch, and encouragement.
- Say two yesses for every no.
- Provide a variety of things for the child to experience.
- Refrain from interrupting child when possible.

- Refrain from interpreting the child's behavior. "You like looking at yourself in the mirror."
- Instead, report the child's behavior. "Judy is looking in the mirror."
- Respond when child initiates play.
- Take care of own needs.
- For additional helpful parent behaviors see *Help! for Parents of Children Six to Eighteen Months.*[5]

*5. Unhelpful parent behaviors*

- Fails to provide protection.
- Restricts mobility.
- Criticizes or shames child for exploring or for anything.
- Discipline or punishment.
- Expects child not to touch "precious" objects.
- Expects toilet training.
- Discounting.

*6. Clues to a need for adults to grow up again*

- Boredom.
- Reluctance to initiate.
- Being overactive or overquiet.
- Avoiding doing things unless you can do them perfectly.
- Being compulsively neat.
- Not knowing what you know.
- Thinking it is okay not to be safe, supported, protected.

*7. Activities that support growing up again*

- Use and adapt this stage's "Helpful parent behaviors" to care for your inner child.
- Explore your house on your hands and knees. Notice how different things look.
- Ask a friend to take you some place you have never been before.
- Explore some safe objects. Shake, smell, taste, look at, listen to, stack the objects. Pay close attention to the objects. Think how you feel when you devote yourself to learning about familiar things in a new way.
- Explore new talents, foods, activities, and cultures.
- Drive to work a different way.
- Get therapy if you need it.

*8. Growing up again affirmations for exploring (when you feel ready)*

- I explore and experiment and I get support and protection while I do.
- I use all of my senses when I explore.
- I do things as many times as I need to.
- I know what I know.
- I am interested in everything.
- I like to initiate and grow and learn.
- I love and accept myself when I am active and when I am quiet.

Doing

**You can explore and experiment and I will support and protect you.**

6 - 18 mos.

Doing

**You can use all of your senses when you explore.**

6 - 18 mos.

Doing

**You can do things as many times as you need to.**

© J.I. Clarke

6 - 18 mos.

Doing

**I love you when you are active and when you are quiet.**

6 - 18 mos.

## Stage Three — Thinking from about 18 Months to about 3 Years

In order to separate from parents, children must learn to think and solve problems. Learning to express and handle feelings is also important. These lessons are the focus of Stage Three — the "thinking" stage.

*1. Job of the child (developmental tasks)*

- To establish ability to think for self.
- To test reality, to push against boundaries and other people.
- To learn to think and solve problems with cause and effect thinking.
- To start to follow simple commands.
- To express anger and other feelings.
- To separate from parents without losing their love.
- To start to give up beliefs about being the center of the universe.
- To continue tasks from earlier stages.

*2. Typical behaviors of the child*

- Begins cause and effect thinking.
- Starts parallel play.
- Starts to be orderly, even compulsive.
- Sometimes follows simple commands, sometimes resists.
- Tests behaviors: "No, I won't, and you can't make me."
- Some try out the use of tantrums.

*3. Affirmations for thinking*

- I'm glad you are starting to think for yourself.

- It's okay for you to be angry, and I won't let you hurt yourself or others.
- You can say no and push and test limits as much as you need to.
- You can learn to think for yourself and I will think for myself.
- You can think and feel at the same time.
- You can know what you need and ask for help.
- You can become separate from me and I will continue to love you.

*4. Helpful parent behaviors*

- Affirm the child for doing developmental tasks.
- Continue to offer cuddling, love, safety, and protection.
- Celebrate the child's new thinking ability.
- Encourage cause and effect thinking.
- Provide reasons, how to's, and other information.
- Accept positive and negative expression of feelings.
- Teach options for expressing feelings instead of hitting or biting.
- Set reasonable limits and enforce them.

- Remain constant in face of child's outbursts; neither give in nor overpower.
- Provide time and space for child to organize thinking.
- Give simple, clear directions child can follow; encourage and praise achievement.
- Expect child to think about own feelings and start to think about other's feelings.
- Think of and refer to child as a "Terrific Two."
- Take care of own needs.
- For additional helpful parent behaviors, see *Help! for Parents of Children 18 Months to 3 Years.*[6]

*5. Unhelpful parent behaviors*

- Using too many don'ts and not enough do's.
- Getting caught in power struggles.
- Trying to appear to be a good parent by having a compliant child.
- Referring to the child as a "terrible two."
- Refusing to set limits or expectations.
- Setting too high expectations.
- Expecting child to play "with" other children before learning to play "near" others.
- Refusing to use discipline for not thinking.
- Shaming the child.
- Discounting.

*6. Clues to a need for adults to grow up again*

- Inappropriate rebelliousness (chip on shoulder).
- Rather be right than successful.
- Bullying, and use of anger to cover fear or sadness.

- Think the world revolves around self.
- Fear of anger in self or others.
- Saying no or yes without thinking.
- Scared to say no and allows others to dominate.
- Passive-aggressive behaviors.

*7. Activities that support growing up again*

- Use and adapt this stage's "Helpful parent behaviors" to care for your inner child.
- Make a "No List" of things it is important for you to say no to and say no to them.
- Get a new recipe or something to assemble. Follow directions exactly. Get three people to tell you how well you did.
- Do something to improve your memory. Learn about memory, read a book, take a workshop, practice. Pick seven things it is important for you to remember and remember them.
- Learn to use a Fuss Box. (See "The Fuss Box," Appendix A.)
- Get therapy if you need it.

*8. Growing up again affirmations for thinking (when you feel ready)*

- I think for myself and I let others think for themselves.
- It's okay for me to be angry, and, when I am, I express it in a way that helps solve problems and does not hurt myself and others.
- I say no whenever I need to say no.
- I can think and feel at the same time; I use my feelings to help me think clearly about what to do.
- I know what I need and I ask for help whenever I need it.
- I am separate from others and I love them and am loved by them.

### Stage Four — Identity and Power
### From about 3 to about 6 Years

The tasks of this stage focus on learning and activities that help the person establish an individual identity, learn skills, and figure out role and power relationships with others.

*1. Job of the child (developmental tasks)*

- To assert an identity separate from others.
- To acquire information about the world, himself, his body, his sex role.
- To learn that behaviors have consequences.
- To discover his effect on others and his place in groups.
- To learn to exert power to affect relationships.
- To practice socially appropriate behavior.
- To separate fantasy from reality.
- To learn what he has power over and what he does not have power over.
- To continue learning earlier developmental tasks.

*2. Typical behaviors of the child*

- Engages in fantasy play, possibly with imaginary companions.
- Gathers information: how, why, when, how long, et cetera.
- Tries on different identity roles by role playing.
- Starts learning about power relationships by watching and setting up power struggles.
- Practices behaviors for sex role identification.
- Starts cooperative play.
- Practices socially appropriate behavior.
- Begins interest in games and rules.

*3. Affirmations for identity and power*

- You can explore who you are and find out who other people are.
- You can be powerful and ask for help at the same time.
- You can try out different roles and ways of being powerful.
- You can learn the results of your behavior.
- All of your feelings are okay with me.
- You can learn what is pretend and what is real.
- I love who you are.

*4. Helpful parent behaviors*

- Affirms children for doing developmental tasks.
- Continues to offer love, safety, and protection.
- Is supportive as child continues to explore the world of things, people, ideas, feelings.
- Encourages child to enjoy being a boy, or a girl; teaches that both sexes are okay.
- Expects child to express feelings and to connect feelings and thinking.

- Provides information about child's environment and corrects misinformation.
- Gives answers to questions.
- Provides appropriate positive or negative consequences for actions.
- Uses language that is clear about who is responsible for what. (See "Encouraging Responsibility through Language," Appendix A.)
- Encourages child's fantasies and his separation of fantasy and reality.
- Compliments appropriate behavior.
- Maintains contact with supportive people who help parent nurture self.
- Responds matter of factly and accurately to child's curiosity about the human body, and the differences between boys and girls.
- Resolves their own identity problems that surface.
- For additional helpful parent behaviors, see *Help! for Parents of Children 3 to 6 Years.*[7]

5. *Unhelpful parent behaviors*

- Teasing.
- Inconsistency.
- Not expecting child to think for self.
- Unwillingness to answer questions.
- Ridicule for role playing or fantasies.
- Respond to child's fantasies as if real.
- Use of fantasy to frighten or confuse child.
- Discounting.

6. *Clues to a need for adults to grow up again*

- Having to be in a position of power.
- Afraid of or reluctant to use power.
- Unsure of personal adequacy.
- Identity confusion — needing to define self by a job or relationship.

- Feeling driven to achieve.
- Overuse of outlandish dress or behavior.
- Frequently comparing yourself to others and needing to come off better.
- Wanting or expecting magical solutions or effects.

7. *Activities that support growing up again*

- Use and adapt this stage's "Helpful parent behaviors" to care for your inner child.
- Make a list of ten things you would like to do.
- Give or go to a costume party.
- Join a men's group if you are a man or a women's group if you are a woman. Talk and think about your idea of sex roles.
- Find out about a different job or career.
- Write a story starting, "In my next life I will . . ."
- Learn about appropriate manners to use in another culture.[8]
- Get therapy if you need it.

8. *Growing up again affirmations for identity and power (when you feel ready)*

- I continue to explore who I am and I find out who other people are instead of making assumptions.
- I am powerful and I do ask for help whenever I need it.
- I try out new roles and I learn new ways of being effective and powerful.
- I accept responsibility for the results of my behavior.
- I feel, accept, and act appropriately on all of my feelings.
- I differentiate between reality and fantasy.
- I love who I am.

## Stage Five — Structure
## From about 6 to about 12 Years

It's important at this stage to learn more about Structure and install our own internal Structure. This includes understanding the need for rules, the freedom that comes from having appropriate rules, and the relevancy of rules. Examining the values on which our rules are based is important. Another major task of this stage is acquiring many kinds of skills.

### 1. Job of the child (developmental tasks)

- To learn skills, learn from mistakes, and decide to be adequate.
- To learn to listen in order to collect information and think.
- To practice thinking and doing.
- To reason about wants and needs.
- To check our family rules and learn about structures outside the family.
- To learn the relevancy of rules.
- To experience the consequences of breaking rules.
- To disagree with others and still be loved.
- To test ideas and values and learn value options beyond the family.
- To develop internal controls.
- To learn what is one's own responsibility and what is others' responsibility.
- To develop the capacity to cooperate.
- To test abilities against others.
- To identify with same sex.
- To continue to learn earlier tasks.

### 2. Typical behaviors of the child

- Asks questions and gathers information.
- Practices and learns skills.
- Belongs to same sex groups or clubs.
- Compares, tests, disagrees with, sets, breaks, and experiences consequences of rules.
- Challenges parent values, argues, and hassles.
- May be open and affectionate or seem cantankerous, self-contained, or may alternate among these.

### 3. Affirmations for structure

- You can think before you say yes or no and learn from your mistakes.
- You can trust your intuition to help you decide what to do.
- You can find a way of doing things that works for you.
- You can learn the rules that help you live with others.
- You can learn when and how to disagree.

124

- You can think for yourself and get help instead of staying in distress.
- I love you even when we differ; I love growing with you.

4. *Helpful parent behaviors*

- Affirm the child for doing developmental tasks.
- Continue to offer love, safety, and protection.
- Affirm children's efforts to learn to do things their own way.
- Give lots of love and lots of positive strokes for learning skills.
- Be a reliable source of information about people, the world, and sex.
- Challenge behavior and decisions; encourage cause and effect thinking.
- Be clear about who is responsible for what.
- Affirm children's ability to think logically and creatively.
- Offer problem-solving tools.
- Set and enforce needed non-negotiable and negotiable rules.
- Allow children to experience non-hazardous natural consequences for their ways of doing things.
- Point out that you do continue to care for them even when they disagree with you.
- Encourage the separation of reality from fantasy by encouraging children to report accurately.
- Be responsible yourself and encourage the children to be responsible for their decisions, thinking, and feeling. (See "Encouraging Responsibility through Language," Appendix A.)
- Encourage children's skill development by providing in the area of

their interest: first, a teacher who is encouraging and enthusiastic, then one who teaches skills and insists on quality performance; still later, probably not until adolescence, one who acts as model and mentor.[9]
- For additional helpful parent behaviors, see *Help! for Parents of Children 6 to 12 Years.*[10]

5. *Unhelpful parent behaviors*

- Uneven enforcement of rules.
- Insisting on perfection.
- Expecting child to learn needed skills without instructions, help, or standards.
- Filling all of the child's time with lessons, teams, and activities so child lacks the unstructured time to explore interests and learn the relevancy of rules.
- Unwillingness to allow child to feel miserable for brief times.
- Rules and values too rigid or lacking.
- Unwillingness or lack of ability to discuss beliefs and values, to reevaluate rules, and to expect the child to develop skills for personal responsibility.
- Discounting.

6. *Clues to a need for adults to grow up again*

- Having to be part of a "gang."
- Only functioning well as a loner.
- Not understanding the relevance of rules.
- Not understanding the freedom that rules can give.
- Unwillingness to examine own values or morals.

- Needing to be king or queen of the hill.
- Trusting the thinking of the group more than one's own thinking and intuition.
- Expecting to have to do things without knowing how, finding out, or being taught how.
- Being reluctant to learn new things or be productive.

### 7. Activities that support growing up again

- Use and adapt this stage's "Helpful parent behaviors" to care for your inner child.
- Join a club and figure out what the rules are.
- Watch TV for one evening and list the morals and values presented. Compare the number of alcoholic drinks, cups of coffee or tea, soft drinks, water, incidents of violence, incidents of nurturing, et cetera.
- Clean and organize something — closet, drawers, sewing kit, tool kit.
- Learn a new system of organization.
- Learn a new skill.
- Get therapy if you need it.

### 8. Growing up again affirmations for developing Structure (when you feel ready)

- I think before I say yes or no and I learn from my mistakes.
- I trust my intuition to help me decide what to do.
- I find a way of doing things that works for me.
- I know the rules that help me live with others and I learn new ones in new situations.
- I know when and how to disagree.
- I think for myself and get help instead of staying in distress.
- I am lovable even when I differ with others; I love growing with others.

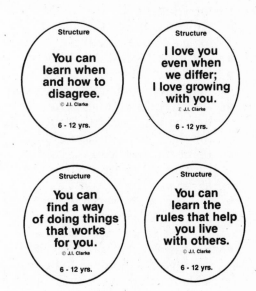

Structure

**You can think before you say yes or no and learn from your mistakes.**
© J.I. Clarke
6 - 12 yrs.

Structure

**You can trust your intuition to help you decide what to do.**
6 - 12 yrs.

Structure

**You can learn when and how to disagree.**
© J.I. Clarke
6 - 12 yrs.

Structure

**I love you even when we differ; I love growing with you.**
© J.I. Clarke
6 - 12 yrs.

Structure

**You can find a way of doing things that works for you.**
© J.I. Clarke
6 - 12 yrs.

Structure

**You can learn the rules that help you live with others.**
© J.I. Clarke
6 - 12 yrs.

**Stage Six — Identity, Sexuality
and Separation
From about 13 to about 19 Years**

The tasks of this stage focus on identity, separation, and sexuality.

*1. Job of the adolescent (developmental tasks)*

- To achieve a clearer separation from family.
- To take more steps toward independence.
- To emerge gradually, as a separate, independent person with own identity and values.
- To be responsible for own needs, feelings, behaviors.
- To integrate sexuality into the earlier developmental tasks.

*2. Typical behaviors of the adolescent*

Adolescents make some of their identity and separation choices by revisiting or recycling the tasks of earlier stages — Being, Doing, Thinking, Identity and Power, and Structure — with new information and with the sometimes confusing pressures of their emerging sexuality.

Therefore, adolescents may act very grown up one moment and immature the next. The ages at which they usually recycle and incorporate these earlier tasks are as follows:*

Onset of puberty or about age thirteen, recycling the Being and the Doing or Exploratory stages of infancy:

- Sometimes independent and sometimes wanting to be fed and cared for.
- Exploring new areas without necessarily being concerned with standards or finishing.

Age fourteen, recycling two and independent thinking:

- Sometimes reasonable and competent with intermittent rebellious outbursts.

Age fifteen, sixteen, and seventeen, recycling three, four, or five, and Identity and Power:

- Asking questions, "Why?" and "How come?" Working out new role identity with same sex and opposite sex with both peers and adults. Learning to solve complex problems.

Age sixteen through nineteen, recylcing six to twelve years, and Structure.

- Being adult and responsible with sudden short journeys back to earlier rule-testing behaviors.
- May also break rules as part of separation from parent.

---

* Thanks to Pamela Levin for identifying these ages and stages.

*3. Affirmations for identity, separation, and sexuality*

- You can know who you are and learn and practice skills for independence.
- You can learn the difference between sex and nurturing and be responsible for your needs, feelings, and behavior.
- You can develop your own interests, relationships, and causes.
- You can learn to use old skills in new ways.
- You can grow in your maleness or femaleness and still be dependent at times.
- I look forward to knowing you as an adult.
- My love is always with you. I trust you to ask for my support.

*4. Helpful parent behaviors*

- Affirm the adolescent for doing developmental tasks.
- Continue to offer love, safety, and protection.
- Accept all of the adolescent's feelings and talk about what it was like when you had emerging sexual feelings.
- Confront discounting.
- Identify the ways the adolescent is becoming separate and affirm the ones that are supportive of his independence.
- Understand and affirm his reworking of tasks from earlier developmental stages.
- Celebrate his growing up and welcome him to adulthood.

- Encourage his growing independence and accept the identity that he is forging, urging him to "be who he is" and to find accommodations with socially acceptable behaviors. This may be different from the parent's expectations or dreams for him.
- For additional helpful parent behaviors, see *Help! for Parents of Children of Teenagers*.[11]

*5. Unhelpful parent behaviors*

- Uses unresponsive, uncaring behavior.
- Withholds loving touch.
- Responds sexually to adolescent's developing sexual maturity.
- Uses rigid rules or no rules or unevenly enforced rules or refusal to negotiate rules.
- Neglects to expect thinking and problem-solving behavior.
- Cruelly teases about sexuality, interests, fantasies, dreams, appearance, or friends.
- Fails to confront destructive or self-defeating behaviors — anything from drug abuse to limited friends and interests.
- Attempts to keep child from separating.
- Unwilling to allow child to feel miserable for brief times.
- Discounting.

*6. Clues to a need for adults to grow up again*

- Preoccupation with sex, body, clothes, appearance, friends, sex role.

- Unsure of own values; vulnerable to peer pressure.
- Problems with starting and ending jobs, roles, and relationships.
- Overdependence on or alienation from family and others.
- Irresponsibility.
- Trouble making and keeping commitments.
- Looks to others for definition of self.
- Confuses sex with nurturing.
- Unsure of maleness or femaleness or lovableness.

*7. Activities that support growing up again*

- Use and adapt this stage's "Helpful parent behaviors" to care for your inner child.
- Write an essay starting: "What I want most to accomplish in my life is . . ."
- Do something for a cause you believe in.
- Have a long talk with a mentor about what is important to you.
- Get a new hairstyle, some new clothes, a new look.
- Go to a romantic movie or play or read a sexy novel.
- Separate from a person who hurts you.
- Join a support group.
- Get therapy if you need it.

*8. Growing up again affirmations for identity, separation, and sexuality (when you feel ready)*

- I know who I am and I know how to be independent.
- I get my nurturing needs met and I get my sexual needs met and I do both of those in a responsible way.
- I continue to evaluate and develop my interests, relationships, and causes.
- I learn new ways to use old skills.
- I continue to grow in my maleness or my femaleness, and to update my roles.
- I am dependent when I need to be, and I ask for support when I need it.
- I grow up again.
- I love myself; I am my own best friend.

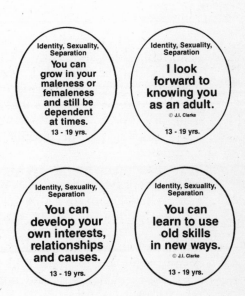

Identity, Sexuality, Separation — **You can grow in your maleness or femaleness and still be dependent at times.** 13 - 19 yrs.

Identity, Sexuality, Separation — **I look forward to knowing you as an adult.** © J.I. Clarke 13 - 19 yrs.

Identity, Sexuality, Separation — **You can know who you are and learn and practice skills for independence.** 13 - 19 yrs.

Identity, Sexuality, Separation — **You can learn the difference between sex and nurturing and be responsible for your needs and behavior.** 13 - 19 yrs.

Identity, Sexuality, Separation — **You can develop your own interests, relationships and causes.** 13 - 19 yrs.

Identity, Sexuality, Separation — **You can learn to use old skills in new ways.** © J.I. Clarke 13 - 19 yrs.

## Young Adults Living at Home

Parenting does not stop at nineteen or twenty-one or ever. A parent is always a parent. The way that parents offer and accept support changes through the decades, but the love and caring does not end.

For many young adults there is a transition stage of both dependence and independence, when they are not yet financially or perhaps fully emotionally independent adults, so they need to live at home. This stage is made more difficult for the young adults if their parents treat them as children, to cook, clean, and do laundry for them, to support them financially with no expectation that they provide for part of their expenses, or to demand that they rigidly adhere to rules established during their teen years.

It is helpful for parents and young people to remember some things about each other.

- Parents are still expected to set non-negotiable rules about any area of lifestyle that is crucial to their values and beliefs, and young people must comply as long as they remain at home.
- Most rules can and should be negotiated.
- It is usually better to anticipate needs, set or negotiate rules as well as plan initial labor divisions before the arrangement is finally agreed upon.
- It is usually better not to make any assumptions about who will do what, but to ask about and negotiate all tasks.

- It is okay for parents to help their grown children as long as the help does not marshmallow or indulge the young adult and as long as the parents do not resent it.
- It is all right for young adults to live with parents, to pay room and board, to share fully in household tasks, and to participate with the same consideration and courtesy they would if they were living with some other family.

- It is helpful for parents to be aware that there are four ways young people separate from parents.

  1. Some leave home and return grown up.
  2. Some stay home and grow up.
  3. Some leave and come back several times.
  4. Some break family rules so their parents will force them to leave.

The way a young person chooses to leave may be different from the way the parents used. The important issue is not how young people leave, but that they do become separate adults, capable of making their own decisions, and willing to interact with their parents as supportive adults.

- It is important for parents to encourage their children to become adults and to treat them as such no matter where they are living.

- It is important for young adults to let their parents grow up, to see, experience, and treat their parents as growing people and not to cling to the images they had when they were four or nine or seventeen years old.
- It is all right for young adults to parent their parents in areas where the young adults have information necessary to help their parent.
- It is wonderful for both young adults and their parents to realize that these years can be a source of satisfaction and enjoyment while they discover each other as caring adults.
- It can be an ideal time for both young adults and parents to do some important growing up again.

## Stage Seven — Interdependence
## Adults

The developmental tasks of adulthood focus on the journey from independence to interdependence, and include regular recycling of earlier tasks in ways that support the specific adult tasks.*

*1. Job of the adult*

- To master skills for work and recreation.
- To find mentors and to mentor.
- To grow in love and humor.
- To offer and accept intimacy.
- To expand creativity and honor uniqueness.
- To accept responsibility for self and to nurture the next generation and the last.
- To find support for one's own growth and to support the growth of others.
- To expand commitments beyond self and family to the community, the world, and possibly beyond.[12]
- To balance dependence, independence, and interdependence.
- To deepen integrity and spirituality.
- To refine the arts of greeting, leaving, and grieving.
- To accommodate aging and accept dying.

---

\* Thanks to Pamela Levin for describing and naming the process of recycling. You can read more about it in her book, *Becoming the Way We Are*.

*2. Behaviors of the adult*

There are many behaviors typical of the long years of the adult stage. The important ones for you right now are the ones you are doing; so list behaviors that are typical for you now.

_____

_____

_____

_____

_____

*3. Affirmations for adults*

- Your needs are important.
- You can be uniquely yourself and honor the uniqueness of others.
- You can be independent and interdependent.
- Through the years you can expand your commitments to your own growth, to your family, your friends, your community, and to all humankind.
- You can build and examine your commitments to your values and causes, your roles, and your tasks.

- You can be responsible for your contributions to each of your commitments.
- You can be creative, competent, productive, and joyful.
- You can trust your inner wisdom.
- You can say your hellos and good-byes to people, roles, dreams, and decisions.
- You can finish each part of your journey and look forward to the next.
- Your love matures and expands.
- You are lovable at every age.

*4. Helpful adult behaviors*

- Affirm developmental tasks.
- Willingness to look at self with love, objectivity, and forgiveness.
- Willingness to celebrate successes, however large or small.
- Willingness to grow and change.
- All behaviors that support the fulfillment of the affirmations.

*5. Unhelpful adult behaviors toward self*

- Resistance.
- Unwillingness to learn, grow, and change.
- Competition with others for emotional needs.
- Imposing own definition of the world on others.
- Passivity, addiction, and codependency.
- Discounting.

*6. Clues to a need for adults to do growing up again tasks from the adult stage.*

- Overdependency.
- Afraid to be dependent.

- Independence to the exclusion of interdependence.
- Difficulty making and keeping commitments.
- Role inflexibility.
- Afraid to grow old.
- Unwilling to say hello and good-bye.
- Unwilling to grieve and then move on with life.
- Living in the past.
- Living in the future.
- Living through others.
- Not knowing or getting what you need.
- Denial and discounting.
- Codependency.

*7. Activities that support growing up again*

There are two types of activities that support growing up again. One is to identify episodes from adult life and redo them, making new decisions and claiming new attitudes about who we are. The other is to do the growing up again for each earlier developmental stage as many times as necessary.

**A. General Activities for Growing Up Again**

One way to do this is to respond to the anxieties, needs, or clues that we identify in our daily lives, to notice the developmental stage they may spring from, and to use the affirmations and activities that support growing up again in that stage.

Another way to grow up again is to pick a theme and choose activities to help recycle that theme at each developmental stage. Here are some examples of themes:

- Knowing what I know.
- Knowing that I need nurturing and accepting it.
- Being willing to be seen and valued.
- Being responsible for myself and to others.
- Building strong, not rigid, boundaries.

Here are some of the ways Eric explored the "Knowing what I know" part of the Stage One (Being) developmental chart.

- A couple of times each week he chose three or four activities he thought would support just "being."
- He gave himself the affirmations for that stage and arranged for other people to take care of him and to give him the affirmations in the way that he wanted them.
- He focused on just being and on knowing what he knew about his body.
- He thought about how his body felt during and after each activity.
- He got a therapeutic massage.
- He soaked in a hot tub; he wandered around aimlessly; he listened to soft music.
- He got lots of hugs and back rubs from his family.

- He drank cocoa and hot cider; he looked at his baby pictures; he visualized himself as a wonderful infant; he exercised when he felt like it, and took naps or rested when he was tired.

Sometimes we can use our intelligence and ingenuity to create these experiences for ourselves in our daily living. Sometimes we get the help we need in a book such as Muriel James' *Breaking Free, Self-Reparenting for a New Life*.[13] Sometimes we need the help of a respectful, caring support group. Sometimes we need the help of a therapist and a therapy group.

The ability to intellectualize is the strength and hazard of the adult stage. The temptation to avoid doing healing, feeling work, and body work is important to recognize as a signal that we need loving help in order to deal with our old defenses.

We also can benefit from finding new parent figures to mentor and nurture us. Muriel James has suggested that we need many good fathers and many good mothers, many smart people to think with, and many people to play with, and they don't all have to be the same people.

We may choose a "new parent" therapist as described in Jonathan and Laurie Weiss's book, *Recovery from Codependency: It Is Never Too Late to Have a Happy Childhood*[14] — or we may contract with other people to play limited new parent roles with us.

## B. Growing Up Again by Revising Specific Episodes

The other type of activity that supports growing up again is to identify specific events in adult life, do them over again, let go of old negative feelings and decisions, and keep the new, positive, good ones. For example:

- There were several unfortunate happenings surrounding Genevieve and Charlie's wedding, so they are going to do their wedding over again and have it be the way they want this time.
- Barbara has regrets about events on her fortieth birthday so she is going to give herself a fortieth birthday party on an unbirthday date.
- Beth harbors bad feelings about the way she was fired from her job so her support group is going to role-play a job termination that is respectful. Beth will indicate what she wants to have happen.
- Sometimes we can't think of a way to do things over so we have to use other methods. Ted wants to resolve his feelings about his experiences in the Vietnam War. He has found a therapy group created specifically to help veterans grieve and heal from their war and post-war experiences.

When you do an adult growing up again experience, it is important to let the new feelings and lessons in, to make new and healthy decisions about yourself and your life. Often, doing this about an episode in adult life is healing and satisfying. Other times, it seems to be not enough. That often means we need to go to an earlier developmental stage to do some additional healing there.

*8. Affirmations for starting to grow up again*

Anytime we make changes in what we believe or how we behave, we must keep several things in mind. First, people around us may not be enthusiastic about our changes. They may be more comfortable with us the way we are now. They may try hard to get us not to change or to thwart our efforts to change. Nonetheless, get the support you need and persist.

Second, we may not always be enthusiastic about the changes ourselves. This is especially true if we jump into them and don't take time to honor and grieve our old decisions as we replace them with new ones.

**Here are some affirmations for starting to grow up again**

- It's okay to start today.
- It took me a long time to build the defenses I have built. I can take time to heal. Healing any weak spot strengthens other weak spots.
- I can welcome feeling stuck as a signal that the next healing is especially important and has a wonderful new freedom waiting.
- I have all the courage I need; the more I use, the more I have.
- I am worth the effort.

Rest assured that as you make necessary changes, when you realize you have said or done something you regret, you can apologize and do it again in a healthier way. As the old carpenter said, "I'd rather work with wood. I can shave it and shim it and get it to work for me." Shim and shave your words and behaviors. Make them work for you. An "I'm sorry I said what I said yesterday, I'm going to try again" can help. Solving problems or resolving differences means making the effort and making some mistakes, acknowledging them, learning from them, and repairing them now.

Rest assured that you will run into a few surprises in the journey ahead. You may celebrate some, grieve some, honor some. Looking at both the past and the present for useful information is necessary in order to create a better present and future. Avoiding, denying, and blaming keeps you in a painful present and assures a painful future.

Rest assured that the notion of living a life free of discord, conflict, and difficulty is a myth. Those who subscribe to this myth inflict pain on themselves and others. Take the path of courage. Be tenacious and be willing to give and receive love.

We want to assure you that it's all worth it. We have kept a sign on our writing desk that says, "The woods would be very silent if only those birds sang who sang the best." So sing! One day at a time.

# *Tools for Family Growth*

## ASKING FOR CHANGE
### *(to be used with page 38)*

All of us have to ask other people to change their behaviors or attitudes from time to time. How effective we are may depend on how many ways we have of asking. Here are eleven ways to ask people to change. Having eleven choices does not guarantee success, but it does increase our chances of being effective. Any of these eleven ways, if delivered in a loving, firm, nonthreatening voice, can build self-esteem and send the message, *you are lovable and capable.* The first six are helpful for enforcing rules. The remaining five can be used to encourage responsible behavior and attitudes.

Here is a description of each way and two examples of each. The first example is addressed to a teenager who is driving too fast. The second example is addressed to someone who doesn't keep promises well.

### Help for Enforcing Rules
### *1. Give direction*
*Description:* Directions should be clear. Directions that describe a state of being are not helpful; for example, "Be a good girl." Instead, use statements that describe behavior such as, "Remember to say please and thank you."

*Examples:*

- "Stop speeding. You are risking your safety and the safety of others. Drive within the speed limit."
- "Keep your promise."

### 2. Offer a reminder of a rule, a contract, or a promise

*Description:* When you offer a reminder, you make a statement that is designed to encourage the listener to think, to remember, and to act.

*Examples:*

- "Remember the rules about safe driving."
- "You made me a promise on Thursday about my birthday."

### 3. Offer a choice of two things

*Description:* This technique is often referred to as "the grandma question," as in "Are you going to dress yourself or shall I dress you?" when staying in pajamas is not an option. The two items offered should be somewhat parallel and should not involve a threat. The options are limited and encourage compliance or obedience.

*Examples:*

- "Are you willing to stay within the speed limit, or shall I drive today?"
- "You promised to sweep the garage today. Are you going to do that this morning or this afternoon?"

### 4. State an expectation

*Description:* Offer a simple but explicit statement of expected behavior.

*Examples:*

- "You are important to me. I expect you to drive safely."
- "I'm depending on you to keep your promise."

### 5. Demand with a consequence

*Description:* A demand with a consequence is usually thought of as being a directive, "Shape up," followed by a negative consequence, "or ship out." It can also have a positive consequence: "Keep up your studies as you have been and you will make the dean's list."

*Examples:*

- "Drive within the speed limit. Any time that you exceed it you will lose the use of the car for the weekend."

- "Break your promise and I will be mad at you!" or "Keep your promise and I will be very proud of you!"

### 6. *Warn of outcome*

*Description:* A warning is a reminder to think about the possible outcomes, positive or negative, of a behavior or an attitude.

*Examples:*

- "Think about what happens to people who often drive over the speed limit. Is that what you want for yourself?"
- "If you continue to break your promises to me, I will not feel like trusting you."

## Help for Encouraging Responsibility

### 7. *Offer to help*

*Description:* Offer to help in a general or a specific way. Avoid offering to take responsibility away from the person.

*Examples:*

- "I'm scared about your safety when you speed. Do you want me to help you in some way?"
- "Do you want ideas from me on how to handle the promise you made?"

### 8. *Make a request*

*Description:* A request is a question that begins with words that imply "Will you," or "Are you willing to . . ." or "Is someone willing to . . ." Use *only* when both affirmative and negative answers are acceptable. Asking, "Will you set the table now?" and receiving "no" for an answer and then saying, "Well, set it anyway," is crooked and crooked questions encourage crooked responses.

*Examples:*

- "Will you drive more slowly?"
- "You promised to go to the movie with us tonight. Do you still intend to go?"

### 9. *Report a feeling*

*Description:* Report a negative or a positive feeling and relate it to a behavior. Own the feeling. Say, "I feel . . ." Do not project it on to the other person with a "You make me feel . . ."

*Examples:*

- "When you drive this fast I feel scared."
- "I'm glad you kept your promise to me."

## 10. Report a wish

*Description:* Tell a specific behavior you wish the person would do. Avoid generalities such as, "I wish you would do better," or "I wish you would be a good girl."
*Examples:*

- "I wish you would drive within the speed limit."
- "I wish you would value yourself enough to take your promises seriously."

## 11. Offer or elicits three or more options

*Description:* This method involves making several suggestions or inviting the other person to identify several options, thus moving beyond the either/or thinking of the "grandma question."
*Examples:*

- "I hear you say that driving fast is fun. What are six safe things you can do that are fun?"
- "You have not been keeping your promises lately. Let's think what you could do. You could continue to break them and deal with the consequences. You could stop making promises you don't intend to keep. You could do more things when the need arises so you aren't in a position to make so many promises. What options can you think of?"

Not all eleven ways will be suitable for all situations. Notice that "make a request" and "report a wish" would not be safe choices to use with the speeding teenager.

**Family Activities**

Ask family members to identify the three ways each would most like to be asked to make changes.

For a specific behavior, write an example of each of the eleven ways. Choose the one that is most likely to be effective. Try it out. If it doesn't work, try another one.

## USING CONTRACTS
*(to be used with pages 32, 40)*

Contracts can be a very helpful tool for starting new behavior in a family. Contracts can be initiated by a child or parent when the underlying desire of both is to work together to get a problem solved.

When you have developed a verbal contract with a child who is six or older, it is sometimes helpful to put the contract in visual form. Use symbols, pictures, drawings, or this written contract form.

**Contract**

**Mutual Goal or Problem** *John doesn't have clean clothes to wear to school.*

| | Child<br>John, age 10 | Parent<br>Mom |
|---|---|---|
| *Background*<br>Describe current situation or behavior | *Loans clothes and toys to others and doesn't get them back. Runs short of clothes between wash days.* | *Wants John to wear clean clothes to school.* |
| *Change*<br>Describe desirable situation or behavior | *Will stop lending school clothes. May lend toys at his discretion.* | *Will not "bug" John about his clothes and toys not being at home.* |
| *Benefit*<br>Of proposed behavior change | *Learns to say "no" to friends and be responsible for his clothes. Learns consequences of loaning toys.* | *Will not have to buy new clothes to replace loaned ones. Will not be mad at John.* |
| *Effort/action*<br>When, where, what, how, how long | *Will be sure he understands which clothes are school clothes. Will not loan school clothes. Will select several items of older clothes he can loan.* | *Will not remind John or "bug" him. Will see that John has adequate school clothes and will wash them regularly.* |
| *Support Solicited* | *Mom and Dad will compliment John on his successes at weekly family meeting.* | *John will compliment Mom and Dad at the meeting for not bugging him.* |
| *Rewards*<br>Positive consequences, celebrations | *When John and Mom have kept the contract for two weeks, they will play miniature golf to celebrate.* | |
| *Penalties*<br>Negative Consequences | *John has to pay for lost school clothes from his allowance and make up the difference by doing yard work or errands.* | *Mom does one of John's chores for a week or buys him a new T-shirt.* |

## CREATIVE HASSLING

*(to be used with pages 39, 47)*
A Form of Distant Intimacy
Excerpted from the book, *Creative Hassling*
by Sally Dierks, reprinted with permission

Creative hassling is one enjoyable way to spend time with a youngster, provide support, and be intimate and distant at the same time. Since school age and adolescent children touch their parents less than they did as little children, they need to find new ways to be connected, to have intimacy but still have their social distance. Some children do this by hassling.

### What Is Creative Hassling?

Creative hassling is a way for parents to interact with children that is assertive and affirming, challenging and rewarding, cooperative and fun. Use it when you want to connect playfully around an issue or a point of conflict. The five steps in hassling are:

- invitation,
- acceptance,
- hassle,
- closure, and
- celebration.

Hassling includes restating negative communications into positive ones, calling attention to grandiosities, and stimulating alternative thinking in a supportive, healthy manner.

A prerequisite for creative hassling is that the adult is willing to stay in charge of the creative hassling process, is willing to spend time hassling, and does it with caring for self and the other person. Accept this role only when you are willing to provide a nurturing climate and an umbrella of protection and respect, and you are willing to listen, to enjoy bantering, and to be willing to accept bantering in return. By doing this, you allow the youngster time to explore ideas, check consequences and be on the same social level with you. Another prerequisite of creative hassling is that both people understand that winning is not the goal. The goal is intimacy, a distant form of intimacy.

Creative hassling is suitable for use *only after responsibilities have been established*. It is not a way to establish rules. How responsibilities are carried out can be a topic for hassling.

144

Assume your thirteen-year-old son has the task of fixing lunch for this week. A creative hassling episode might go like this:

| | | |
|---|---|---|
| Invitation | Mother: | Will you fix lunch now? |
| Acceptance | Son: | I'm not going to eat lunch now. |
| | Mother: | Fix lunch for the rest of us anyhow. |
| Hassle | Son: | How come I always have to fix lunch? |
| | Mother: | Always? Every day of your life? (Grabs son around waist, rubs his back) How long do you want to hassle? Five minutes? Ten minutes? What kind of hassling do you want? |

The two do a little body jostling, each being careful not to hurt the other.

| | |
|---|---|
| Son: | You're pulling on my skin! |
| Mother: | How come my skin doesn't stretch like that? How come you are so good looking? |
| Son: | Cuz I got such a good-looking, smart mother. |
| Mother: | We are two good-looking smart people aren't we? |
| Son: | Too smart to fix lunch now. |
| Mother: | Too smart not to fix lunch now. |
| Son: | I should have quit while I was behind. |

| | | |
|---|---|---|
| Closure | Both: | Laugh |
| | Mother: | Will you fix lunch now? |
| | Son: | Yeah. |
| | Mother: | Thank you. I enjoyed hassling with you. |

What has just happened? The mother and son have spent some pleasurable time together, had acceptable body contact, and acknowledged the already established rules.

## Preliminary Questions to Ask Yourself about Creative Hassling

1. Are you, the adult, willing to spend some time doing creative hassling?
2. Will you be conscious of your own feelings and have fun?

(when you stop having fun, stop creative hassling, and enforce the rule or solve the problem).
3. Are your own rules or family responsibilities clear?
4. Are you willing to listen?
5. Are you willing to set aside logic temporarily and play with alternatives, even the ridiculous ones?

If the answer to each of the above questions is yes, you are ready to begin the process.

## Process of Creative Hassling

1. Initiate hassling.
2. Listen for acceptance.
3. Keep tangible objects or behaviors, not feelings, the object for hassling.
4. Assume that all statements made have a positive, caring meaning.
5. Redefine or restate negative sounding statements into positive ones.
6. Have fun with grandiose statements.
7. Push alternatives and flexible thinking.
8. Affirm the personal importance of yourself and your child. Identify both of you as winners.
9. Close creative hassling with a statement of appreciation for the other person.

Creative hassling, in addition to providing intimacy, may be used to avoid power struggles, but it is only effective on the days when both people are willing to engage in it.

# SAMPLE RULES CHARTS

*(to be used with pages 40, 55)*

Families need to have rules that are clear and posted for all to see. Not posting rules invites confusion and manipulation. It is easier to challenge and change a posted rule to suit the needs of family members.

There are two types of rules that help families be successful. One set applies to interactions with others and respect for self. The other applies to jobs and responsibilities around the house. The items on these lists are suggestions and examples. Use the rules that fit for your family and add the ones you need.

## People Rules

1. Think and feel for yourself.
2. Tell the truth. Say yes when you mean yes and no when you mean no.
3. Figure out what you need.
4. Ask clearly for what you need and want.
5. Respect and be helpful to yourself and others.
6. Affirm yourself and others.
7. Be responsible for your behavior.
8. Cooperate.
9. _____
10. _____

## House Rules

1. Make your bed before breakfast.
2. Put your dirty clothes in the hamper right after you take them off.
3. Clean your room by Saturday noon.
4. Finish your yard chores by Saturday at four o'clock.
5. Set the table for dinner by six o'clock or finish the dishes within one hour after dinner.
6. _____
7. _____

## THE FUSS BOX
*(to be used with pages 44, 121)*

Using a Fuss Box is a quick way to honor the energy that anger generates and to harness that energy for problem solving. A Fuss Box is not useful for reducing deep rage about times of hurt from years past. That rage is often best dealt with in therapy.

The Fuss Box is a tool that can be used when anger is interfering with solving a problem or when one's mind keeps dwelling on an irritation. "Stuffed" or denied anger only comes back to haunt us later, in physical symptoms or in contaminated thinking.

Anger, like all other emotions, is a signal to us, a piece of information about what is going on. Denying anger cuts us off from important information. Hanging on to anger keeps us stuck in the feeling. Expressing the anger frees us to solve problems.

Sometimes people can express anger in words at the time the anger occurs. Other times it is not wise to express one's anger, so we must find another way. Sometimes people can breathe deeply six times and let the angry feeling go. Other times people need to complain, scream, fuss, or let the anger out physically by playing racquetball or hitting a punching bag. When we use any of these methods it is important to begin problem solving after releasing the anger.

Using a Fuss Box takes from three to five minutes. Think through the ground rules and contract with yourself to fuss vigorously but briefly, and always to follow the fussing with problem solving.

The purpose of the Fuss Box is to help people

- claim their right to be angry,
- have a way to express anger without hurting themselves or other people, and without other people interfering with it or trying to "fix" it,
- claim responsibility for resolving their anger,
- get information from their feelings, and
- use their energy to get on with solutions to the problem.

## How to Use a Fuss Box

1. Stand in a sturdy cardboard box.
2. Fuss. Say anything you want to; exaggerate if you want to.
3. Kick the box if you want to.
4. Feel your energy switch from angry to calm.
5. Step out of the box.
6. Decide at least one thing you will do to make the situation better and do it.

## Precautions

1. Select with care the place where you will use the box. Only use it when you are alone or in a place where people care about you and will not interrupt or try to placate you and are not the objects of your fussing. Do not use it in front of children who are under two years old. Using it in front of children two or older teaches them that anger is a signal that there is a problem and that people are to express anger in harmless ways and turn their anger energy into problem solving.
2. Do not use the Fuss Box just to vent anger or frustration and then do nothing about the situation. That would be using the box to hold on to your anger and to make life worse instead of better.

## GETTING FREE OF DOUBLE BINDS
*(to be used with page 99)*

### What Is a Double Bind?

A double bind is a set of two or more messages, each of which is or seems to be true when given separately, but when given in combination are contradictory, create a problem and elicit confusion, anger, rage, fear, or helplessness. The messages may be:

● Verbal and given simultaneously. Heather says, "Tell me all about your weekend right now, but I have to leave in five minutes."

● Verbal and nonverbal given simultaneously. Heather says, "Tell me all about your weekend right now," and then she walks out of the room.

● Verbal or nonverbal, given at different times — Heather says, "I want to hear all about your weekend soon. I'm interested!" During the next six months you offer to tell about the weekend four times. Each time Heather proclaims her interest but won't take time for the conversation.

### Examples of Double Binds

"I love you." / "Don't inconvenience me."
"Be successful." / "Be dependent."
"Grow up." / "Don't grow up."
"Be unique." / "Do it my way."
"Be perfect." / "Don't be better than I am."
"Always please others." / "Stand up for yourself."

### How to Counter Double Binds and
### Resolve the Problems They Create

Think of a double bind you have received or choose one from the list above to practice on. Answer each of the following questions.

1. Is my relationship or contract with the person who offered this bind an important one? Shall I ignore both messages and just walk away from this or do I need to deal with it somehow?
2. If I need or want to deal with it, what is my goal? (For example, my goal is to keep my job.)
3. Can I reach my goal by confronting the double message? Would it be wise to say to the person, "That's silly. I can't go two ways at once. Pick one"?
4. If that would not be wise, is there something in one of the messages that I can use to help me reach my goal? If there is, can I ignore or circumvent the other message? Can I respond to the other message in a small, non-destructive way?
5. If this relationship or situation is important and none of the above questions help identify a way to resolve the double bind, it may be time to ask this question: Is this bind unimportant or do I need to be building a new relationship or looking for a new situation?

### Children and Double Binds

Children, as well as adults, need skills for dealing with double binds. Because double binds are so immobilizing, they give rise to strong feelings. Children need help with their feelings and with thinking about what to do. Parents can:

- Teach children what double binds are and about the destructiveness of double binds.
- Teach children to identify options for resolving the dilemmas that double binds create.
- Let children hear and see the parents deal with double binds.
- Encourage children to point out double binds so parents can replace conflicting words and behaviors with loving Nurture and clear Structure.
- Teach children to honor their feelings and to use them to help recognize double binds.

Because double binds elicit more than one feeling, asking children to tell you how they feel may be less effective than helping them sort through their feelings with exercises like this next one.

### The Feeling Faces Board —
### Let Your Finger Do the Talking*

Use the balloon faces on the "Ups and Downs with Feelings" faces board,* page 154.

- Tell your child you are going to play a faces game to help learn how to deal with double binds.
- Say a double bind to your child ("I love you." / "I ignore you.") Ask him to point to the face or faces that show how he feels when you say those together. Mark or record which of the faces the child points to for later reference. Don't worry about naming the feelings at this time. Young children don't have many names for feelings.
- Say one of the messages, "I love you." Ask him to point to the faces that show how he feels when he hears that message alone. Mark the face(s).
- Say the other message, "I ignore you." Ask him to point to the face(s) that show how he feels when he hears that message alone. Mark the face(s).
- Tell him that people have feelings to help them know what to do and that double binds are confusing, partly because we have more than one feeling about them.
- Teach him that when he feels sad he is to get comfort. When he feels scared, he is to move to a safe place or get help from someone. When he is glad, he is to enjoy his gladness and maybe share it with someone else. When he is angry, he is to think how to get what he needs. When he is confused and needs more information, he is to get it. When he feels a mix of emotions he may be dealing with a double bind.
- Go back over the faces he pointed to and help him identify his needs and get comfort, safety, celebration problem-solving ideas, information, or whatever is appropriate for each one. If you want to teach names for the emotions, this is a good time to do it.

When your child is facing a double bind dilemma with friends or at school, you can use the "Ups and Downs with Feelings" faces board (page 154) and the questions previously described to help him feel, think, and decide what to do, and perhaps to help you decide how to give him further support.

---

* Thanks to Carole Gesme for permission to reproduce the faces board from her series of games, "Ups and Downs with Feelings." Reprinted with Permission.

## How Adults Can Reclaim the Ability to Recognize Feelings

Some adults who grew up with double binds learned to cope with them by ceasing to feel their confusion and by acting as if double binds are normal. As adults, these people will not have developed skills for protecting themselves from the destructive dilemmas of double binds and will probably give them without noticing it. One way adults can help themselves reclaim their feelings is by using their fingers to show them what their heads have had to forget. What the head had to forget, the body remembers, so if you are such a person, you can use the faces board to help you reclaim your feelings. You can do this alone, with a partner, or in a support group. Don't use the word "feeling" or worry about naming the feeling. Just ask your finger to point to the face that shows how it was when he told you he loved you, or when he was drunk, or when she said he wasn't drunk, he was sick, or when she said it was your fault.

You can use the information your finger gives you to think about what you needed then and what you need to be aware of now.

## Change Double Binds to Congruent Messages

As you think about double binds and reclaim your feelings about them, you will become more aware of giving them. If you think you may have set up a double bind, you can ask the person who received it if it felt like a double bind. You can think about whether the messages really do conflict, or you can pretend you are getting the messages and use the faces board to let your fingers do the talking. If, in fact, you have offered a double bind, take action to remove it and give clear, congruent messages about what you want.

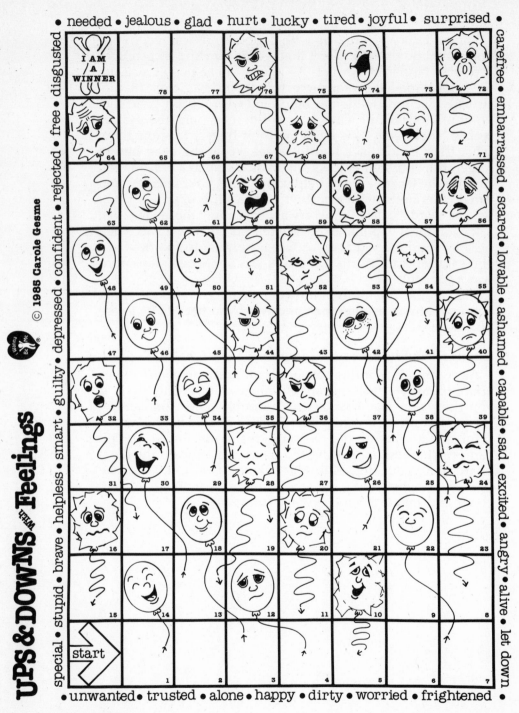

UPS & DOWNS with Feelings

© 1985 Carole Gesme

I AM A WINNER

start

needed • jealous • glad • hurt • lucky • tired • joyful • surprised •

carefree • embarrassed • scared • lovable • ashamed • capable • sad • excited • angry • alive • let down •

special • stupid • brave • helpless • smart • guilty • depressed • confident • rejected • free • disgusted •

• unwanted • trusted • alone • happy • dirty • worried • frightened •

154

## ENCOURAGING RESPONSIBILITY
## THROUGH LANGUAGE

*(to be used with pages 105, 123, 125)*

Encouraging responsibility in children is an important part of parenting. Becoming even more responsible for getting our needs met and for empowering others is an important part of growing up again for adults.

Parents can use these six guidelines for responsible language to help them act responsibly, to teach children to be responsible, and to grow into independence. Making a habit of speaking responsibly will help to move a family away from unhealthy enmeshment or codependence and into healthy caring, independence, and interdependence.

### Guidelines that Support Responsible Language

1. Ask directly for what you want or need.
2. Think and feel for yourself, not for others.
3. Be responsible for your own feelings and be responsive to the feelings of others.
4. Say "yes" and "no" straight.
5. Remember that people, not things, are responsible for behavior.
6. Respond to questions with straight answers.

Here are the six guidelines for responsible communication. Listed alongside them are irresponsible or codependent ways of communicating. Each principle is especially important when going through or recycling the developmental stage listed here and described in Section Four.

### Stage One

| **Responsible:** | **Irresponsible:** |
|---|---|
| 1. Ask directly for what you want or need. Say what is to be done and who is to do it. | Imply that someone should do something, manipulate. |
| *Examples:* | *Examples:* |
| "Will you give me something to drink?" "Come and eat lunch now." "Do you have money to deposit in our checking account today?" | "I'm thirsty." "The soup is getting cold." "The checkbook is overdrawn." |

### Stage Two

| **Responsible:** | **Irresponsible:** |
|---|---|
| Think and feel for yourself, not for others. | Think and feel for others. |
| *Examples:* | *Examples:* |
| "I like this. Do you like it?" "What do you think of this?" "I am offended by that." | "You are going to love this." "You will not approve of this." "I know you mean to be kind, but. . ." |

### Stage Three

| **Responsible:** | **Irresponsible:** |
|---|---|
| Be responsible for your own feelings and responsive to the feelings of others. | Attempt to make others responsible for your feelings and ignore or redefine theirs. |
| *Examples:* | *Examples:* |
| "I am furious." "I feel wonderful." "Here is what we are having for dinner. I hope you enjoy it." | "You make me so mad!" "You make me happy." "I know you don't like the food I cook, but do eat it just to please me." |

## Stage Four

**Responsible:**

Say yes and no straight and don't ask "Will you..." unless you are willing to accept either yes or no for an answer.

*Examples:*

"Will you set the table?" "No, not tonight." "Have you finished your project?" "No, it won't be ready until tomorrow." "Do you want me to help you?" "Yes, please."

**Irresponsible:**

Be indirect. Manipulate.

*Examples:*

"Will you set the table?" "I might do it later." "Have you finished your project?" "I didn't know that you wanted it today." "Do you want me to help you?" "Oh, you are busy and I'm all right."

## Stage Five

**Responsible:**

Remember that people, not things, are responsible for behavior.

*Examples:*

"What did you do today?" "I see that we are nearly finished." "You may be able to use the ideas in this book."

**Irresponsible:**

Act as if what people are responsible for is beyond their control.

*Examples:*

"How did your day go?" "Things are falling into place." "This book will solve your problem."

### Stage Six

| **Responsible:** | **Irresponsible:** |
| --- | --- |
| Respond to questions with straight answers. (Stage Six) | Don't reveal yourself. Manipulate. |
| *Examples:* | *Examples:* |
| "Where are your boots?" "I left them at work." "How much money do you need?" "I need fifteen dollars." "Do you have time to help me for half an hour?" "Not today, but I can tomorrow if you still need me." | "Where are your boots?" "I'm not going to wear them today." "How much money do you need?" "I don't need it until later." "Do you have time to help me for half an hour?" "Why?" |

*Self-Esteem: A Family Affair Leader Guide* by Jean Illsley Clarke has six exercises that can be used in groups to help people practice recognizing irresponsible language and using responsible language.

# *Tools for Personal Growth*

## DEVELOPMENTAL AFFIRMATIONS: HOW TO USE THEM WITH YOUR FAMILY AND YOURSELF
*(to be used with pages 73, 114-18,
120-24, 126, 128-29, 132, 134, 162-165)*

When we offer developmental affirmations to children, we offer powerful support that strengthens their ability to accomplish their developmental tasks successfully.

Unfinished business from any prior developmental stage will demand to be addressed again until the child resolves it satisfactorily, so it is important to offer the affirmations from preceding stages as well as those corresponding to a child's current age. As adults, we are continually recycling previous stages from day to day so all fifty-four affirmations (see pages 162-165) are appropriate for us.

Explore these affirmations. Copy them. Cut them out. Color them: red for age 0 - 6 months, orange for 6 - 18 months, yellow for 18 months to 3 years, green for 3 to 6 years, light blue for 6 to 12 years, dark blue for 13 to 19 years, and lilac or purple for the adult years. Post them. Read them. Say them. Listen to them.

Pay attention to how you give affirmations. Remember to offer the affirmations to other people as *"I* care about *you"* or *"You* can grow at your own pace" messages. Only when they have thought about and decided to trust the messages should they change it to *"I* care about *myself"* or *"I* (*do*) grow at my own pace."

Read the affirmations to yourself, *"You can* grow at *your* own pace," speaking as your own nurturing parent to the child within. Your child may not believe you at first and may have to test and observe you before being able to say wholeheartedly, "It is okay for *me* to grow at *my* own pace," or *"I do* grow at my own pace." If we hurry the use of "I" in affirmations, we are only adding one more layer of adaptive behavior — one more layer of letting other people tell us how to think, feel, and do.

Here are several ways to use the affirmations with children, yourself, and other adults. These exercises are from the book, *Affirmation Ovals: 139 Ways to Give and Get Affirmations* by Jean Illsley Clarke and Carole Gesme.

### 1. Finding Affirmations to Help You Identify What You Need

Read each affirmation and put the ones that sound especially good to you in a separate pile. Then read those and ask yourself what they have to do with what's going on in your life at the moment. Decide how you will get what you need based on this very personal assessment.

### 2. Introducing the Affirmations to Children Who Do Not Read

Put the affirmations in a basket. Ask a child to get the basket and hand you an affirmation. Read it to him. Continue as long as the child shows interest in the activity or until all affirmations have been read.

### 3. Pairs*

Use this exercise with any pair of people who have some commitment to each other, couples, colleagues, siblings, or parent and child, for example, and use the affirmations to find out what people want and need from each other. Give each person a set of the ovals. Ask each to arrange the set in front of herself by color rows; then look at each row and pick which

---

* Thanks to Gail and Harold Nordeman for designing this activity.

messages she wishes the other person would give her. Go through chosen messages with the other person. Ask:

- "Did you know this person wants this affirmation from you?"
- "Do you give it now?"
- "How?"
- "If the other person isn't hearing, seeing, or getting that, how else can you give it?"
- "If you don't believe you can give it, what do you need that will enable you to give it? How can you get that?"
- "Will you give the affirmation right now?"
- (To the person who wishes to receive the affirmation) "Do you accept this? Anything else you need?"

### 4. Ask Your Family**

Sitting in a circle with Affirmation Ovals spread in front of them, each person in the family picks one, two, or three affirmations and asks the family member from whom he would like to hear each message to read it. If that person does not want to give the affirmation, the family can think about what each of them needs and if they need to improve their Structure and rules so there is room for more love and self-esteem in the family.

### 5. Good-Night (Especially for kids)***

Keep a basket of Affirmation Ovals by each child's bed. Let the child pick three each night. Say those to the child as you tuck him into bed.

### 6. Helping Teenagers****

Picture your teenager when she was very young. As she grew, visualize what was going on at each developmental stage in her life and yours. If there were affirmations from any stage that you didn't know about or give, give them now. Use the color-coded affirmations as your guide. Give them verbally, tell your child what was going on at that time, then give the ovals. She may act as if she doesn't care or she may scoff. Give them anyway.

---

** Thanks to Jean Koski for designing this activity.
*** Thanks to Julie Thomas for designing this activity.
**** Thanks to Linda Buranen for designing this activity.

### 7. Problem Solving

Have each person think of a problem that he needs or wants to solve. He identifies three possible solutions and chooses affirmations that will be helpful in resolving this problem.

### 8. You Can't Go Back but You Can Get What You Need Now

Work in pairs. Tell your partner a short story about a typical day in your life when you were a certain age or the age your child is now. Include your name and nicknames, your family, house, school, friends, not-friends, activities, sports, what you liked to do, what you did well, and what your wishes were.

Lay out all of the affirmations up to and including the age you are telling about. Pick up the affirmations that would have helped you on the kind of day you described. Take as many affirmations as you want. Of those, pick the most important three or four or the ones that feel best to you today. Have your partner read them to you, once with your eyes open, and your partner handing them to you one at a time, and once again with your eyes closed.

*color these ovals red*

**Being**

**I'm glad you are alive.**

J.I. Clarke

Birth - 6 mos.

**Being**

**You belong here.**

J.I. Clarke

Birth - 6 mos.

**Being**

**What you need is important to me.**

J.I. Clarke

Birth - 6 mos.

**Being**

**I'm glad you are you.**

J.I. Clarke

Birth - 6 mos.

**Being**

**You can grow at your own pace.**

J.I. Clarke

Birth - 6 mos.

**Being**

**You can feel all of your feelings.**

J.I. Clarke

Birth - 6 mos.

**Being**

**I love you and I care for you willingly.**

J.I. Clarke

Birth - 6 mos.

*(for instructions on Affirmation Ovals, see page 159)*

*color these ovals orange*

**Doing**
You can explore and experiment and I will support and protect you.
6 - 18 mos.

**Doing**
You can use all of your senses when you explore.
6 - 18 mos.

**Doing**
You can do things as many times as you need to.
© J.I. Clarke
6 - 18 mos.

**Doing**
You can know what you know.
© J.I. Clarke
6 - 18 mos.

**Doing**
You can be interested in everything.
© J.I. Clarke
6 - 18 mos.

**Doing**
I like to watch you initiate and grow and learn.
© J.I. Clarke
6 - 18 mos.

**Doing**
I love you when you are active and when you are quiet.
6 - 18 mos.

*color these ovals yellow*

**Thinking**
I'm glad you are starting to think for yourself.
18 mos. - 3 yrs.

**Thinking**
It's OK for you to be angry and I won't let you hurt yourself or others.
18 mos. - 3 yrs.

**Thinking**
You can say no and push and test limits as much as you need to.
© J.I. Clarke
18 mos. - 3 yrs.

**Thinking**
You can learn to think for yourself and I will think for myself.
© J.I. Clarke
18 mos. - 3 yrs.

**Thinking**
You can think and feel at the same time.
© J.I. Clarke
18 mos. - 3 yrs.

**Thinking**
You can know what you need and ask for help.
© J.I. Clarke
18 mos. - 3 yrs.

**Thinking**
You can become separate from me and I will continue to love you.
18 mos. - 3 yrs.

*color these ovals green*

**Identity and Power**
You can explore who you are and find out who other people are.
3 - 6 yrs.

**Identity and Power**
You can be powerful and ask for help at the same time.
3 - 6 yrs.

**Identity and Power**
You can try out different roles and ways of being powerful.
3 - 6 yrs.

**Identity and Power**
You can find out the results of your behavior.
3 - 6 yrs.

*(for instructions on Affirmation Ovals, see page 159)*

*color these ovals green*

**Identity and Power**

**All of your feelings are OK with me.**
© J.I. Clarke

3 - 6 yrs.

**Identity and Power**

**You can learn what is pretend and what is real.**
© J.I. Clarke

3 - 6 yrs.

**Identity and Power**

**I love who you are.**
© J.I. Clarke

3 - 6 yrs.

*color these ovals light blue*

**Structure**

**You can think before you say yes or no and learn from your mistakes.**

6 - 12 yrs.

**Structure**

**You can trust your intuition to help you decide what to do.**

6 - 12 yrs.

**Structure**

**You can find a way of doing things that works for you.**
© J.I. Clarke

6 - 12 yrs.

**Structure**

**You can learn the rules that help you live with others.**
© J.I. Clarke

6 - 12 yrs.

**Structure**

**You can learn when and how to disagree.**
© J.I. Clarke

6 - 12 yrs.

**Structure**

**You can think for yourself and get help instead of staying in distress.**

6 - 12 yrs.

**Structure**

**I love you even when we differ; I love growing with you.**
© J.I. Clarke

6 - 12 yrs.

*color these ovals dark blue*

**Identity, Sexuality, Separation**

**You can know who you are and learn and practice skills for independence.**

13 - 19 yrs.

**Identity, Sexuality, Separation**

**You can learn the difference between sex and nurturing and be responsible for your needs and behavior.**

13 - 19 yrs.

**Identity, Sexuality, Separation**

**You can develop your own interests, relationships and causes.**

13 - 19 yrs.

**Identity, Sexuality, Separation**

**You can learn to use old skills in new ways.**
© J.I. Clarke

13 - 19 yrs.

**Identity, Sexuality, Separation**

**You can grow in your maleness or femaleness and still be dependent at times.**

13 - 19 yrs.

**Identity, Sexuality, Separation**

**I look forward to knowing you as an adult.**
© J.I. Clarke

13 - 19 yrs.

**Identity, Sexuality, Separation**

**My love is always with you. I trust you to ask for my support.**

13 - 19 yrs.

*(for instructions on Affirmation Ovals, see page 159)*

*color these ovals lilac or purple*

Interdependence

**You can be creative, competent, productive and joyful.**

Adult

Interdependence

**You can trust your inner wisdom.**

Adult

Interdependence

**You can say your hellos and goodbyes to people, roles, dreams and decisions.**

Adult

Interdependence

**You can finish each part of your journey and look forward to the next.**

Adult

Interdependence

**Your love matures and expands.**

Adult

Interdependence

**You are lovable at every age.**

Adult

Interdependence

**Your needs are important.**

Adult

Interdependence

**You can be uniquely yourself and honor the uniqueness of others.**

Adult

Interdependence

**You can be independent and inter-dependent.**

Adult

Interdependence

**Through the years you can expand your commitments to your own growth, to your family, your friends, your community and to all humankind.**

Adult

Interdependence

**You can build and examine your commitments to your values and causes, your roles and your tasks.**

Adult

Interdependence

**You can be responsible for your contributions to each of your commitments.**

Adult

*(for instructions on Affirmation Ovals, see page 159)*

## SEEING OUR OWN SHIELDS — A VISUALIZATION

*(to be used with page 110)*

This is a visualization. It is a way to get a picture of your ability to care for yourself and others. If you are a person who does not see pictures in your head easily, you can try doing the exercise anyway. You can imagine what your picture would look like. Remember that however it looks is okay because it is *your* shield *today*. Record the following directions onto a cassette tape, reading slowly, and listen to them, or ask someone to read them slowly to you.

Seat yourself comfortably or lie down. Check out the various parts of your body to be sure you are comfortably situated. Keep your body straight, without crossed arms or legs.... Close your eyes to shut out the visual distractions.... Now be aware of your hearing.... Listen to the sounds of the room and make them louder.... Now let them go and hear only my voice.... Be aware of your body.... Feel the pressure of your body resting on the chair or the floor.... Feel the air going in and out of your lungs.... Now breathe deeply three or four times....

Become aware that you have something resting lightly at your side.... It does not bother you or distract you and it is always ready to be used.... This object represents your ability to take care of yourself and other people.... Look at it.... It may be a cloak or an umbrella or a bubble of white light or something else. Whatever it is, it's yours so it is right for you. I will call it your shield. It may be the shape of the shields in picture books and museums...or it may look *very* different.... Pick it up.... Feel its weight.... Is it light or heavy?.... Notice the material of which it is made.... Look at its color.... Examine its texture.... Feel its smoothness or roughness.... Tap it with your fingernail.... How does it sound?.... Smell it.... Raise it over your head.... Is it large enough to protect you fully from the rain?.... Can it extend over someone else to protect that person also?... Now hold it in front of you in a position that will deflect the arrows of life.... Notice how well it does that.... Look for holes or thin spots.... There may be a few or there may be many.... They may be large or they may be small.... However your shield is, accept it as it is for you today; it is your shield.... Thank your shield for being there for you and for all of the good work it does for you.... After you have finished appreciating it, place it gently back at your side and become aware once again of your breathing and the sounds and smells around you. Open your eyes when you are ready. (This is the end of the visualization.)

**Follow-up Activities**
1. Write a description of your shield, or draw a picture of it, or describe it to someone.
2. Tell someone about a quality of your shield that you are happy you have developed.
3. Think of one way your shield could be improved.
4. Use the ideas in this book to help you find a way to do that.

**The Great Variety of Shields**

Remembering that your shield is the right one for you, you might like to hear how some other people have described their shields.

"White and loose and fluffy at the edges; can wrap all around me."

"A heavy iron cylinder from my feet to above my head with a small hole to look out."

"A bell of white light."

"A big mahogany bed with a wonderful canopy."

"A canoe shaped to take me through the calm water and the turbulent water."

"New and shiny with a price tag hanging on one side — the price of my recent therapy."

"Thicker over the genitals."

"A semi-permeable membrane that lets love in and keeps hate out."

"Looks great, but it is made of paper."

"Dark and conical and made of lead; it is not crowded inside, but there is no room for anyone else."

"A wall of flowers with thorns to use if I am in danger."

"Cylindrical, enter from one side, protects me all around."

"A wooden lattice or sieve that lets too much through."

"Honey-colored leather, smooth and round with a point in the center. It expands to cover other people."

Whatever your nurturing looks like, honor your ability to care for yourself and others and continue to strengthen it.

## HOW TO FIND A SUPPORT GROUP OR A THERAPIST

Here are some places to find help.

- Twelve Step groups.
- Support groups and therapy groups.
- Individual or family therapy practitioners (counselors, psychologists, psychiatrists, social workers, and other trained and accredited professionals).
- Community mental health centers.
- Churches, hospitals, and crisis telephone lines.

### Twelve Step Groups

Look in your phone book for a number listed under "Alcoholics Anonymous Intergroup or Information Services." Someone there will tell you about meetings in your area. If you live in a smaller town, that office may also have a listing of Adult Children of Alcoholics, Al-Anon, and other Twelve Step meetings available to you.

In a larger city, you may find a phone listing of the Twelve Step group you seek by looking for the group name directly: Overeaters Anonymous, Sex Addicts Anonymous, Parents Anonymous, Fundamentalists Anonymous, and so on.

### Professional Help

One of the best ways to locate a therapist for individual, group, or family therapy is to ask friends and acquaintances for the names of professionals who have helped them. Although a therapist who is just right for another person may not be just right for you, this kind of research is a good way to begin.

If you seek help in recovering from a specific problem such as sexual abuse, you can ask for names of people who specialize in that work. Search out information from YWCA's, YMCA's, counseling centers, and other similar organizations. Ask about the services they provide and ask for referrals to other professionals in your community who may be suited to your needs.

It's okay for you to meet with the professionals and interview one or several before you decide on someone. Ask about their training, experience, and credentials. Ask how they would approach their work with you and what the cost will be. Ask what they expect of you. Pay attention to the information you receive and to your intuition.

When you agree to work with someone, keep several things in mind:

- You may benefit from working with several different helpers. Some people begin in family therapy and move to individual therapy. Some begin with individual therapy and move to group therapy. You and your therapist should discuss the most appropriate help for you at any point in your healing process. The decision is up to you. Trust yourself to know what you know and remember that it is important to get your needs met.
- Sexual contact between a therapist and a client is never okay. If this happens, leave immediately and report the person to her or his professional licensing board or association and get help for this abuse.

Therapy will probably generate discomfort. This discomfort is a necessary part of growing. But if you should feel a particular discomfort about your therapist's behavior, it is important to find out why. Trust your intuition. Your needs are important and you deserve to feel safe.

# ENDNOTES

## Section One

1. Jean Illsley Clarke, Sara Monser, Gail Nordeman, and Harold Nordeman, *Help! for Parents of Teenagers* (San Francisco: Harper & Row, 1986)
2. John Bradshaw, *The Family: A Revolutionary Way of Self-Discovery* (Pompano Beach, Fla.: Health Communications, 1988), 53-54.

## Section Two

1. Alice Miller, *The Drama of the Gifted Child* (New York: Basic Books, 1981); Alice Miller, *Thou Shalt Not Be Aware: Society's Betrayal of the Child* (New York: New American Library, 1984)
2. David Elkind, *The Hurried Child: Growing Up Too Fast Too Soon* (Reading, Mass.: Addison-Wesley Publishing Co., 1981); David Elkind, *All Grown Up And No Place To Go: Teenagers In Crisis* (Reading, Mass.: Addison-Wesley Publishing Co., 1984)
3. Rokelle Lerner, *Daily Affirmations: For Adult Children of Alcoholics* (Pompano Beach, Fla.: Health Communications, 1985)
4. Lynne Williams et al., *The Too Precious Child: the Perils of Being a Super Parent and How to Avoid Them* (New York: Atheneum, Macmillan, 1987)

## Section Three

1. Rollo May, *Power and Innocence: A Search for the Sources of Violence* (New York: C.C. Norton, 1972)
2. Jacqui Lee Schiff et al., *Cathexis Reader: Transactional Analysis, Treatment of Psychosis* (New York: Harper & Row, 1975)
3. Norman Cousins, *Anatomy of an Illness: Reflections on Healing and Regeneration* (New York: W. W. Norton & Company, 1979)
4. Eric Berne, *What Do You Say After You Say Hello?* (New York: Grove Press, 1973), 324-337.
5. William H. Grier, M.D., and Price M. Cobbs, M.D., *The Jesus Bag* (New York: McGraw-Hill, 1971), 1-22.

6. Janet Geringer Woititz, *Adult Children of Alcoholics* (Pompano Beach, Fla.: Health Communications, 1983), 72-73.

7. Robert Subby, *Lost In the Shuffle, The Co-dependent Reality* (Pompano Beach, Fla.: Health Communications, 1987)


**Section Four**

1. Claudia Black, *It Will Never Happen To Me* (Denver, Colo.: M.A.C., 1981)

2. Pamela Levin, *Becoming The Way We Are* (Wenatchee, Wash.: Directed Media, 1985)

3. Jean Illsley Clarke, *Self-Esteem: A Family Affair* (New York: Harper & Row, 1978)

4. Jean Illsley Clarke et al., *Help! For Parents Of Infants From Birth to 6 Months* (San Francisco: Harper & Row, 1986)

5. Jean Illsley Clarke et al., *Help! For Parents Of Children 6 to 18 Months* (San Francisco: Harper & Row, 1986)

6. Jean Illsley Clarke et al., *Help! For Parents Of Children 18 Months to 3 Years* (San Francisco: Harper & Row, 1986)

7. Jean Ilsley Clarke et al., *Help! For Parents Of Children 3 to 6 Years* (San Francisco: Harper & Row, 1986)

8. *Do's And Taboos Around The World,* Parker Pen Company (New York: The Benjamin Company, 1985)

9. Benjamin Bloom, *Developing Talent In Young People* (New York: Ballantine Books, 1985)

10. Jean Illsley Clarke et al., *Help! For Parents of Children 6 to 12 Years* (San Francisco: Harper & Row, 1986)

11. Jean Illsley Clarke et al., *Help! For Parents Of Teenagers* (San Francisco: Harper & Row, 1986)

12. Whitley Streiber, *Communion, A True Story* (New York: Avon Books, 1987); M. Scott Peck, M.D., *The Road Less Traveled* (New York: Simon & Schuster, 1978)

13. Muriel James, *Breaking Free, Self-Reparenting for a New Life* (Reading, Mass.: Addison-Wesley Publishing Company, 1981)

14. Laurie Weiss, and Jonathan Weiss, *Recovery from Co-Dependency:It Is Never Too Late to Have a Happy Childhood* (Pompano Beach, Fla.: Health Communications, 1988)

# SUGGESTED READING

Ackerman, Robert J. *Children of Alcoholics: A Guidebook for Educators, Therapists, and Parents*. Holmes Beach, Fla.: Learning Publications, 1983.

Ackerman, Robert J. *Let Go and Grow: Recovery for Adult Children*. Pompano Beach, Fla.: Health Communications, 1987.

Adams, Caren, Jennifer Fay, and Jan Loreen-Martin. *NO is Not Enough, Helping Teenagers Avoid Sexual Assault*. San Luis Obispo, Calif.: Impact Publishers, 1984.

Andersen, Christopher P. *Father: The Figure and the Force*. New York: Warner Books, 1983.

Badger, Earladeen. *Infant-Toddler: Introducing Your Child to the Joy of Learning*. New York: Instructo/McGraw-Hill, 1981.

Balaban, Nancy. *Learning To Say Goodbye: Starting School and Other Early Childhood Separations*. New York: New American Library, 1985.

Baldwin, Christina. *One To One: Self-Understanding through Journal Writing*. New York: M. Evans, 1977.

Beattie, Melody. *Codependent No More*. Center City, Minn.: Hazelden Educational Materials, 1987.

Bellah, Robert N., Richard Madsen, William M. Sullivan, Ann Swidler, and Steven M. Tipton. *Habits of the Heart: Individualism and Commitment in American Life*. Berkeley, Calif.: University of California Press, 1985.

Bettelheim, Bruno. *A Good Enough Parent*. New York: Alfred A. Knopf, 1987.

Bingham, Mindy. *Minou*. Santa Barbara, Calif.: Advocacy Press, 1987.

Black, Claudia. *Repeat After Me*. Denver, Colo.: M.A.C. Printing & Publications, 1985.

Bolton, Frank G., Jr. *When Bonding Fails: Clinical Assessment of High-Risk Families*. Beverly Hills, Calif.: Sage Publications, 1983.

Bowlby, John. *Attachment*. New York: Basic Books, 1969.

Bowlby, John. *Separation: Anxiety and Anger*. New York: Basic Books, 1973.

Bozarth-Campbell, Alla. *Life is Goodbye, Life is Hello*. Minneapolis, Minn.: CompCare, 1982.

Brown, Stephanie, *Treating Adult Children of Alcoholics: A Developmental Perspective*. New York: John Wiley & Sons, 1988.

Cantwell, Hendrika. *Physical Neglect*. Chicago: National Committee for Prevention of Child Abuse, 1987.

Carnes, Patrick. *The Sexual Addiction.* Minneapolis, Minn.: CompCare, 1983.

Cermak, Timmen L., M.D. *A Primer on Adult Children of Alcoholics.* Pompano Beach, Fla.: Health Communications, 1985.

Crary, Elizabeth. *Kids Can Cooperate: A Practical Guide to Teaching Problem Solving.* Seattle: Parenting Press, 1984.

DiGiovanni, Kathe. *My House Is Different.* Center City, Minn.: Hazelden Educational Materials, 1986.

Faber, Adele, and Elaine Mazlish. *Siblings Without Rivalry.* New York: W. W. Norton & Company, 1987.

Fassler, Joan. *Helping Children Cope: Mastering Stress Through Books and Stories.* New York: The Free Press, 1978.

Forward, Dr. Susan, and Craig Buck. *Betrayal of Innocence: Incest and Its Devastation.* New York: Penguin Books, 1979.

Forward, Dr. Susan, and Joan Torres. *Men Who Hate Women & The Women Who Love Them: When Loving Hurts and You Don't Know Why.* New York: Bantam Books, 1986.

Fossum, Merle A., and Marilyn J. Mason. *Facing Shame: Families in Recovery.* New York: W. W. Norton and Company, 1986.

Freeman, Lory. *It's My Body: A Book to Teach Young Children How to Resist Uncomfortable Touch.* Seattle: Parenting Press, 1982.

Freeman, Lory. *Loving Touches: A Book For Children About Positive, Caring Kinds Of Touching.* Seattle: Parenting Press, 1986.

Friel, John, and Linda Friel. *Adult Children The Secrets of Dysfunctional Families.* Pompano Beach, Fla.: Health Communications, 1988.

Garmezy, Norman, and Michael Rutter. *Stress, Coping and Development in Young Children.* New York: McGraw-Hill, 1983.

Gawain, Shakti. *Creative Visualization.* Mill Valley, Calif.: Whatever Publishing, 1978.

Glenn, H. Stephen and Jane Nelson. *Raising Self-Reliant Children in a Self-Indulgent World.* Rocklin, Calif.: Prima Publishing & Communications, 1988.

Goldberg, Natalie. *Writing Down the Bones: Freeing the Writer Within.* Boston: Shambala Press, 1986.

Gravitz, Herbert L. and Julie D. Bowden. *Guide To Recovery: A Book For Adult Children Of Alcoholics.* Holmes Beach, Fla.: Learning Publications, 1985.

Hagberg, Janet O. *Real Power: Stages of Personal Power in Organizations.* San Francisco: Harper & Row, 1984.

Halpern, Howard M. *How to Break Your Addiction to a Person.* New York: McGraw-Hill, 1982.

Hart, Dr. Louise. *The Winning Family: Increasing Self-Esteem In Your Children & Yourself.* New York: Dodd, Mead & Company, 1987.

Hartman, Cherry. *Be Good To Yourself Therapy.* St. Meinrad, Ind.: Abbey Press, 1987.

Hastings, Jill M., and Marion H. Typpo. *An Elephant in the Living Room: the Children's Book.* Minneapolis, Minn.: CompCare, 1984.

Heffner, Elaine. *Mothering: How Women Can Enjoy a New, Productive Relationship with Their Children and a New Image Of Themselves.* New York: Doubleday Anchor, 1978.

Helfer, Ray E., M.D. *Childhood Comes First, A Crash Course in Childhood for Adults.* East Lansing, Mich.: Ray E. Helfer, 1978.

Johnsen, Karen. *The Trouble with Secrets.* Seattle: Parenting Press, 1986.

Johnson, Spencer, M.D. *The Precious Present.* Millbrae, Calif.: Celestial Arts, 1981.

Kaplan, Louise J. *Adolescence: The Farewell to Childhood.* New York: Simon and Schuster, 1984.

Kaplan, Louise J. *Oneness and Separateness: Infant to Individual.* New York: Simon and Schuster, 1978.

Kaufman, Gershen. *The Dynamics of Power: Building a Competent Self.* Cambridge, Mass.: Schenkman Publishing Co., 1983.

Kaufman, Gershen. *Shame: The Power of Caring.* Cambridge, Mass.: Schenkman Publishing Co., 1985.

King, Lucie A. *How to Encourage Healthy Competition.* Winfield, Ill.: Thunderbird Circle, 1986.

Larsen, Earnie. *Stage II Recovery: Life Beyond Addiction.* San Francisco: Harper & Row, 1985.

Lerner, Harriet Goldhur. *The Dance of Anger.* New York: Harper & Row, 1985.

Loevinger, Jane. *Ego Development.* San Francisco: Jossey-Bass Publishers, 1976.

Magid, M., Carole A. McKelvey, and Ken McKelvey. *High Risk: Children Without a Conscience.* New York: Bantam Books, 1988.

Maxwell, Jean A. *The Teenage Years A Parent's Dilemma.* New Orleans: J. Arthur Systems, 1983.

McConnell, Patty. *Adult Children of Alcoholics: A Workbook for Healing.* San Francisco: Harper & Row, 1986.

Middelton-Moz, Jane Dwinell, and Lorie Dwinell. *After the Tears: Reclaiming the Personal Losses of Childhood.* Pompano Beach, Fla.: Health Communications, 1986.

Miller, Alice. *For Your Own Good: Hidden Cruelty in Child-Rearing and the Roots of Violence.* New York: Farrar, Straus, Giroux, 1983.

Miller, Alice. *Thou Shalt Not Be Aware: Society's Betrayal of the Child.* New York: New American Library, 1984.

Miller, Alice. *The Drama of the Gifted Child: How Narcissistic Parents Form and Deform the Emotional Lives of Their Talented Children.* New York: Basic Books, 1981.

Miller, Jean Baker, M.D. *Toward a New Psychology of Women.* Boston: Beacon Press, 1986.

Missildine, W. Hugh, M.D. *Your Inner Child of the Past.* New York: Pocket Books, 1963.

Nathanson, Donald L., ed. *The Many Faces of Shame.* New York: The Guilford Press, 1987.

Norwood, Robin. *Women Who Love Too Much.* New York: Pocket Books, 1985.

O'Gorman, Patricia A., and Philip Oliver-Diaz. *Breaking The Cycle Of Addiction: A Parent's Guide to Raising Healthy Kids.* Pompano Beach, Fla.: Health Communications, 1987.

O'Gorman, Patricia A. and Philip Oliver-Diaz. *12 Steps to Self-Parenting.* Pompano Beach, Fla.: Health Communications, 1988.

Osherman, Samuel. *Finding Our Fathers.* New York: Free Press, 1986.

Parkes, Colin Murray, and Joan Stevenson-Hinde. *The Place of Attachment in Human Behavior.* New York: Basic Books, 1982.

Patterson, Dr. Francine. *Koko's Kitten.* New York: Scholastic, 1985.

Paul, Dr. Jordan, and Dr. Margaret Paul with Bonnie B. Hesse. *If You Really Loved Me. . .* Minneapolis: CompCare, 1987.

Paul, Dr. Jordan, and Dr. Margaret Paul with Bonnie B. Hesse. *Do I Have to Give Up Me to Be Loved By You?* Minneapolis: CompCare, 1983.

Paul, Norman L., M.D., and Betty Byfield Paul. *A Marital Puzzle: Transgenerational Analysis in Marriage Counseling.* New York: Gardner Press, 1986.

Peck, M. Scott, M.D. *People of the Lie.* New York: Simon and Schuster, 1983.

Peck, M. Scott, M.D. *The Road Less Traveled.* New York: Simon and Schuster, 1978.

Pollard, Dr. John K. *Self Parenting.* Malibu, Calif.: Generic Human Studies Publishing, 1987.

Pruett, Kyle D., M.D. *The Nurturing Father.* New York: Warner Books, 1987.

Reid, Clyde. *Celebrate the Temporary.* New York: Harper & Row, 1972.

Rubin, Lillian B. *Intimate Strangers.* New York: Harper & Row, 1983.

Rubin, Theodore Isaac, M.D. *The Angry Book.* New York: Collier Books, 1969.

Sanford, Linda Tschirhart, and Mary Ellen Donovan. *Women & Self-Esteem.* Garden City, N.J.: Doubleday Anchor, 1978.

Schaeffer, Brenda. *Is It Love or Is It Addiction?* Center City, Minn.: Hazelden Educational Materials, 1987.

Simmermacher, D. G. *Self Image Modification Training.* Pompano Beach, Fla.: Health Communications, 1981.

Smith, Ann W. *Grandchildren of Alcoholics: another generation of co-dependency.* Pompano Beach, Fla.: Health Communications, 1988.

Stinnett, Nick, and John DeFrain. *Secrets of Strong Families.* New York: Berkeley Books, 1985.

Typpo, Marion H., Ph.D., and Jill M. Hastings, *An Elephant in the Living Room: A Leader's Guide for Helping Children of Alcoholics.* Minneapolis, Minn.: CompCare, 1984.

Verny, Thomas. *The Secret Life of the Unborn Child.* New York: Dell Publishing, 1981.

Wegscheider-Cruse, Sharon. *Choice-Making.* Pompano Beach, Fla.: Health Communications, 1985.

Wegscheider-Cruse, Sharon. *Learning to Love Yourself.* Pompano Beach, Fla.: Health Communications, 1987.

Whitfield, Charles L., M.D. *Healing The Child Within.* Pompano Beach, Fla.: Health Communications, 1987.

Whitney, Charlotte. *Win Win Negotiations for Couples: A Personal Guide To Joint Decision Making.* Gloucester, Mass.: Para Research, 1986.

Woititz, Janet Geringer. *Adult Children of Alcoholics.* Pompano Beach, Fla.: Health Communications, 1983.

Woititz, Janet Geringer, Ed.D. *Struggle for Intimacy.* Pompano Beach, Fla.: Health Communications, 1985.

Youngs, Bettie B. *Helping Your Teenager Deal with Stress: A Survival Guide for Parents and Children.* Los Angeles: Jeremy P. Tarcher, 1986.

*Meditation Books by Hazelden Educational Materials:*
*Each Day a New Beginning: Daily Meditations for Women.*
*Today's Gift: Daily Meditations for Families.*
*The Promise of a New Day,* by Karen Casey and Martha Vanceburg.
*The Love Book,* by Karen Casey.
*Touchstones: A Book of Daily Meditations for Men.*
*Night Light: A Book of Nighttime Meditations,* by Amy E. Dean.

# INDEX

## Other Learning Materials Available

**Affirmation Ovals,** laminated, colored ovals are available in pocket, table or wall sizes or as bookmarks. Each set includes all 54 developmental affirmations.

**Affirmation Ovals: 139 Ways to Give and Get Affirmations,** a book by Jean Illsley Clarke and Carole Gesme, is a collection of games and activities to help people of all ages use the affirmation ovals.

The **Sing Yes!** album by Darrell Faires contains six audio cassettes with sixty-three singable, easy-to-remember songs, based on the developmental affirmations. Sung in both male and female voices. Accompaniment tapes included. A sampler of eight songs is also available.

The Developmental Audio Cassette Tapes, **The Important Infants,** children birth to 6 months, **The Wonderful Busy Ones,** children 6 months to 18 months, **Exciting 3 to 6 Year Olds,** present important information about children and the nurturing they need. Told in both male and female voices, the tapes are 12 to 18 minutes long. Listening to each tape daily for three weeks helps the listener incorporate this information to help care for children or for the child within.

The **Ups and Downs With Feelings Games** help children and adults recognize, name, and be responsible for their feelings. The Starter games include a variety of games, a set of affirmation ovals, and a book, **Help! for Parents of Children 3 to 6 years.** The Explorer Games include a set of affirmation ovals, a cloth Feelings Faces game board and, seven games. By Carole Gesme. Separate laminated Feeling Faces posters are also available.

**Ouch, That Hurts, A Handbook for People Who Hate Criticism** is a collection of personal and group activities to help people learn to separate constructive suggestions from criticism and to protect themselves from the slings and arrows of life. By Jean Illsley Clarke.

**Creative Hassling,** a booklet by Sally Dierks, describes the process of Creative Hassling and the theory behind it.

**Growing Up Again Leader's Guide,** write to Daisy Press for information about a guide for leading group meetings based on **Growing Up Again.**

**The Love Game** is a board game for two to four people, age eight and up, that shows a pathway out of shame into celebration by using affirmations of unconditional love.

For information, including prices, write to Daisy Press, 16535 9th Avenue North, Plymouth, MN 55447